Snowshoes, Coaches, and Cross Country Skis

A Brief History of Yellowstone Winters

by Jeff Henry

Roche Jaune Pictures, Inc.

2011

Design and Composition
Jerry Brekke
Livingston, Montana

Cover Photograph by Jeff Henry

Printed and bound in China.
Printed on acid free paper.
Library of Congress Control Number: 2010917621
ISBN 978-0-9679814-0-6
Cloth Bound

First Edition
2011

This book is dedicated to my daughter
Mariah.

Mariah, you are the most beautiful girl
I have ever seen.

Acknowledgements

On January 12, 1806 Captain William Clark wrote a passage in his journal in which he gratefully acknowledged the contributions of George Droulliard, the best woodsman and hunter in Lewis and Clark's Corps of Discovery. Captain Clark wrote: "I scercely know how we Should Subsist, I believe but badly if it was not for the exertions of this excellent hunter...." As Captain Clark appreciated the abilities and efforts of George Droulliard, I have a similar appreciation for the abilities and efforts of Jerry Brekke, my editor and designer for this book. Jerry is the one who navigated the complex technology used to assemble the book, albeit with the excellent counsel of master graphic artist, Mike Dahms. Such an endeavor in my mind is akin to putting together a multi-dimensional jigsaw puzzle, but with the assembly of the puzzle made infinitely more puzzling by today's unfathomable technology. Quite simply, the book would never have come to be without Jerry's acumen, and I will always owe Jerry a great debt of gratitude.

In addition to Jerry Brekke, many other people helped me with this project. I would like to thank Eric Robinson, Mike Keller, Greg Dahling, Victoria Byrd, and Marti Tobias of Xanterra Parks & Resort, Yellowstone. I would also like to thank Bob Crabtree of the Yellowstone Ecological Research Center in Bozeman, Montana for allowing me to use his beautiful map of the Greater Yellowstone Region. Curtis Tierney of Tierney Fine Arts in Bozeman, Montana arranged for me to use a privately owned and wonderful piece of art originally painted by the great Edgar S. Paxson. William Paxson of California furnished biographical information and important images created by his great grandfather, Edgar S. Paxson.

Superb western artist Gary Carter allowed me to use several pieces of his magnificent art, and he remains one of the West's nicest guys. The same could be said for Todd Fredericksen of Gardiner, Montana. Todd also allowed me to use a piece of his art, and as I always say, Todd has unlimited potential and is an immensely gifted artistic talent.

Gary Moulton of the University of Nebraska in Lincoln was quick to answer questions I asked him regarding Lewis and Clark. Mia Merendino, Curator of the Clymer Museum of Art in Ellensburg, Washington was helpful and responsive to my requests. I'd also like to thank the superbly accomplished western art expert Peter Hassrick of the Denver Art Museum, who helped me track down the living descendents of Edgar S. Paxson, and who tried to help me track down information regarding some of John Clymer's paintings.

Fred Watson of the University of California at Monterey put in an enormous amount of time to create the image of an ice-covered Yellowstone during the Pleistocene Glaciation era. Andrew Murray of the British Broadcasting Corps took time out from his insanely busy schedule to arrange for me to use a satellite image of the Yellowstone area that originally appeared in a BBC television programme. Kathy Kasic of Metamorph Films in Livingston, Montana also helped adapt that BBC image to my use.

Sean Campbell of the Buffalo Bill Historical Center in Cody, Wyoming was helpful in arranging for me to use several important images from the Jack Richard collection, which is housed at the BBHC. Phil Cooper and Gregg Losinski of Idaho Fish and Game furnished information about wintering wildlife in the Teton Basin in eastern Idaho. Ken Pierce and Joe Licciardi graciously allowed me to use their overview map of how ice covered the Yellowstone region during the Pinedale Glaciation period.

John Logan Allen allotted a great deal of phone and e-mail time in communicating his thoughts about John Colter. Elizabeth Watry generously furnished me a wealth of information about Beulah Brown. Larry Lahren of Livingston, Montana shared his wealth of knowledge about the prehistory and history of the Yellowstone Homeland.

Steve Tustkanowski-Marsh, Bridgette Guild, Jim Peaco and Molly Conley of the National Park Service were more than helpful in helping me search for and then providing indispensable illustrations from Park Service files in Mammoth and Gardiner. NPS librarians Jackie Jerla and Mariah Robertson were also helpful and more than patient

Last in this list but foremost in terms of his incomparable knowledge of Yellowstone's history as well as in his willingness to help is Lee Whittelsey, Yellowstone National Park Historian. Lee is an extraordinarily busy man with his pursuits in advancing the knowledge of the history of the world's first national park, but he is never too busy to put on hold whatever he is doing to answer a question or to point someone in the proper direction to find what he needs to further his own pursuit. Lee is a public servant in the finest sense, and he seems always to bear in mind that the last word in the title of the bureau he works for is "Service." I owe Lee a great deal of gratitude, and I highly value his friendship.

Abridged Greater Yellowstone Ecosystem Map
Courtesy of the Yellowstone Ecological Research Center

CONTENTS

IMAGE CONTRIBUTIONS

Jeff Henry
British Broadcasting Corporation
Clymer Museum of Art
Edgar S. Paxson
George Catlin
F. Jay Haynes
Gary Carter Western Art
Curtis Tierney • Tierney Fine Art
Todd Fredericksen
David Joaqin
Larry Lahren, Ph.D • Anthro Research
Jerry Brekke
Jack Richard Collection • Buffalo Bill Historical Center

Wim Kolk
Fred Watson, Ph.D
Jerry Bateson, Jr. Collection
Joseph Licciardi, Ph.D
Ken Pierce, Ph.D
Leslie Quinn Collection
Library of Congress
Montana Historical Society
Andrew Langford • National Park Service
Yellowstone National Park Service Library
Yellowstone National Park Service Archives
Yellowstone Ecological Research Center
Yellowstone Gateway Museum

Fred Watson, Ph.D

"At first the greatest accumulations of snow would have
been in the mountain ranges that form a rough ring around the
Yellowstone Plateau. At some point the mountain snow would
have metamorphosed into ice, and glaciers would have started
to flow downhill, onto the central plateaus. This in turn would
have led to a chaotic amalgamation of ice on the plateaus,
where the various montane glaciers collided with each other in
a grinding, heaving struggle for ascendancy."

Yellowstone's Pinedale Glaciation

"A Base 4000 Feet Thick"

© Jeff Henry

Glacial-like countenance of Hayden Valley, sunrise at 35 degrees below zero at Sulphur Springs Creek.

During the last ice age, an event known locally as the Pinedale Glaciation, the area in and around what is now Yellowstone National Park was a far more wintry place than it is today. Indeed, winter at that time would have seemed endless. For 50,000 years an enormous glacier centered on the present park dominated the region, and only superlatives suffice to describe that colossal accumulation of ice. The frozen mass formed a dome that arced over Yellowstone's plateaus and most of its mountains, and measured approximately 100 miles wide from east to west and 160 from north to south. At its thickest point, over Yellowstone Lake, the ice was 4,000 feet deep. From that massive center the thick-

Dr. Fred Watson, California State University, Monterey Bay, produced this concept (facing page) of the massive Pinedale Glacier covering the Yellowstone Plateau and flowing down the Yellowstone River valley into today's Montana. Dome Mountain occupies the left foreground, while the Gallatin Range lies to the right in the image. The Washburn Range rises from the center of the plateau, with the Tetons far in the distance.

Dr. Watson's landscape modeling and ecosystem visualization work has resulted in interpretive, computer-rendered visualizations of ecosystem processes in many protected areas, including Yellowstone National Park.

ness of the ice tapered toward the glacier's margins in the lower elevations surrounding Yellowstone. But also from that central source gargantuan rivers of ice flowed outward, down the major drainages leading away from the Yellowstone high country. The Snake River to the south, the Madison River to the west, and especially the Yellowstone River to the north, each had a tongue of ice as much as 2,500 feet thick that moved irresistibly forward, pressed on by the weight of the ice in the highlands that amounted to as much as 240,000 pounds per square foot.

In the highlands themselves all but the highest peaks were buried under the ice. The glacial mass was so high above the surface of the earth that it created its own weather, raking more snow from passing clouds than the mountains alone could have done. The average annual temperature in central Yellowstone in those days was 15 degrees Fahrenheit, as compared to about 33 degrees today. For tens of thousands of years the massive Yellowstone glacier was to a great degree self sustaining, and if any human observers had been present it would have been logical for them to believe that the glacier would always be.

This most recent glacial chapter began about 70,000 to 80,000 years ago, when for reasons that are not exactly clear the earth's climate experienced a world-wide cooling. Various theories as to why this occurred include a wobbling of the earth's rotation, so that less solar energy was received by the high latitudes in the northern hemisphere. Another theory is that the sun's output diminished for some reason, perhaps due to a change in solar flare activity. Still others suggest that various topographical upliftings around the world altered our planet's weather circulations; volcanic dust blocked solar insolation; or a slight tilting of the earth's axis occurred. Whatever the cause, the cooling was major. Consider that for most of the last 600,000,000 years earth's temperature has averaged 72 degrees Fahrenheit, while today it averages 58 degrees and during the last period of glaciation it was a chilly 50 degrees

In the case of Yellowstone, one of the area's many fire-and-ice ironies predisposed the area to the development of the huge glacier. The upwelling of magma under Yellowstone, the same pool of heat and pressure that has caused the spectacular explosions of the Yellowstone caldera in the past and the same heat source that fuels the park's geothermal wonders today, had pushed the region upward into an elevated plateau long before the earth underwent its general cooling. Because of its high elevation Yellowstone received more precipitation and experienced much cooler temperatures. In a further irony, Yellowstone's past calderic explosions had occurred to the southwest of the park, and had contributed to the formation of the Snake River Valley in what is now southern Idaho. The southwest to northeast orientation of the Snake River Plain, as well as its relatively low elevation, made it a perfect conduit for moisture-laden storms to blow before prevailing southwesterly winds on an unobstructed path to the Yellowstone Plateau, where they dumped their moisture as they rose up and over the highlands.

At first the greatest accumulations of snow would have been in the mountain ranges that form a rough ring around the Yellowstone Plateau. At some point the mountain snow would have metamorphosed into ice, and glaciers would have started to flow downhill, onto the central plateaus. This in turn would have led to a chaotic amalgamation of ice on the plateaus, where the various montane glaciers collided with each other in a grinding, heaving struggle for ascendancy. Ultimate ascendancy came on a stupendous scale, as more and more snow fell and eventually buried the separate flows under one vast ice sheet that only continued to grow in both depth and breadth. The ice field grew until ice backed up the canyons that had spawned the montane glaciers, and then it grew until

it had buried the canyons themselves. And after that the level of the ice rose still higher until it had buried almost all the mountain peaks.

Geologically it all happened very quickly, although by human standards the growth of the ice sheet would have been almost imperceptible. Certainly there must have been variations, exceptionally cold and snowy times when the glacier grew more rapidly, and other times when the weather was warmer or dryer and the glacier grew slowly or perhaps even diminished a bit, but as a rough average, about 12 and a half years were required to accumulate one foot of ice. Although very large in its own right, the Yellowstone glacier was but a footnote when compared to the North American continental glacier that covered virtually all of Canada and the northern United States. The continental glacier extended as far south as the site of present day Great Falls, Montana at its point closest to Yellowstone — it came that close (150 miles) to incorporating the Yellowstone glacier into its far larger mass.

The Yellowstone glacier, like all glaciers, must have subjected itself to unfathomable internal stress and strain, as the enormous weight of the ice pressed down upon itself and forced against surrounding topography. At times fearsome cracks must have opened on the glacier's surface, and then closed again as opposing forces reacted to the resulting open space. Sometimes the outward movement in the rivers of ice flowing from the central glacier was convulsive, as pressure built up behind obstructions or a lull in precipitation relaxed downward force for a time; but when pressure overcame obstruction the outward flow burst forth in a relative surge. In addition to these internal conflicts common to all glaciers, the icy cauldron of the Yellowstone glacier engaged in an ongoing struggle with the area's geothermal and volcanic heat. Some lava flows in the Yellowstone are reputed to be only 70,000 years old. If so, they might have occurred during the existence of the great glacier. Prodigious columns of steam from the meeting of hot lava and ice must have resulted. Imagination also suggests the image of titanic floods of melt water.

Yellowstone's geothermal features were buried under the ice as well. They melted the ice from underneath, and in so doing released rocky debris that the ice had held in suspension. This phenomenon left stoney, gravelly hills in various places in Yellowstone that can be seen today. Usually conically shaped, a good example of these thermal kames, as they are called, can be seen in the Porcupine Hills along Nez Percé Creek on the north edge of Fountain Flats. The low hills on the south side of Rush Lake on the west side of Fountain Flats are another, and the Twin Buttes to the west of the Lower Geyser Basin would be still another.

Even more dramatic would have been the capping of pockets of subterranean geothermal pressure by overlying ice or pools of glacial melt water. When circumstances combined to abruptly release the overlying caps, such as the sudden draining of an overlying glacial lake, these pockets of underground pressure blew off in frightful explosions of steam, water, ice and rock. Resulting steam explosion craters can be seen in many places in Yellowstone today. Mary Bay, Indian Pond and Turbid Lake on the northeast side of Yellowstone Lake are three examples, while Pocket Basin along the Firehole River in the Lower Geyser Basin is another.

Of course, these exceptional surges and upheavals were just that, exceptional. For long periods, the surface of the ice field would have presented itself as a featureless white expanse — similar ice sheets in existence today are often described as the most monotonous landscapes in the world. The Grand Canyon of the Yellowstone, the great geyser basins, Lamar Valley, Hayden Valley, all the hills and streams and plateaus that are held in almost iconic status today were submerged far below the surface of the intransigent ice.

It is almost certain that no human observers were around to witness the Pinedale Glaciation. What is certain is that after dominating the scene for such a long time the great Yellowstone glacier rather abruptly began to melt about 20,000 to 25,000 years ago, and by about 13,000 to 14,000 years ago the Yellowstone Plateau was ice free. Remarkably, the vast volume of ice that had taken 50,000 to 60,000 years to accumulate melted away in a fraction of that time. On a far greater scale, the formation and disappearance of the great Pinedale glaciers followed the pattern of one of today's individual winters, where it takes as much as five months or more to accumulate maximum snowpack, but after warming spring weather reaches a certain tipping point, the snowpack melts away in a much shorter period of time. Following the disappearance of the ice, Yellowstone went through various climatic periods, some of which were warmer and others of which were cooler than the present time. But all those times were similar to the present in that, with some minor exceptions, each summer's weather was warm enough to melt whatever snow had fallen the previous winter. Still, by almost any standards, Yellowstone's winters remained harsh.

Anthro Research

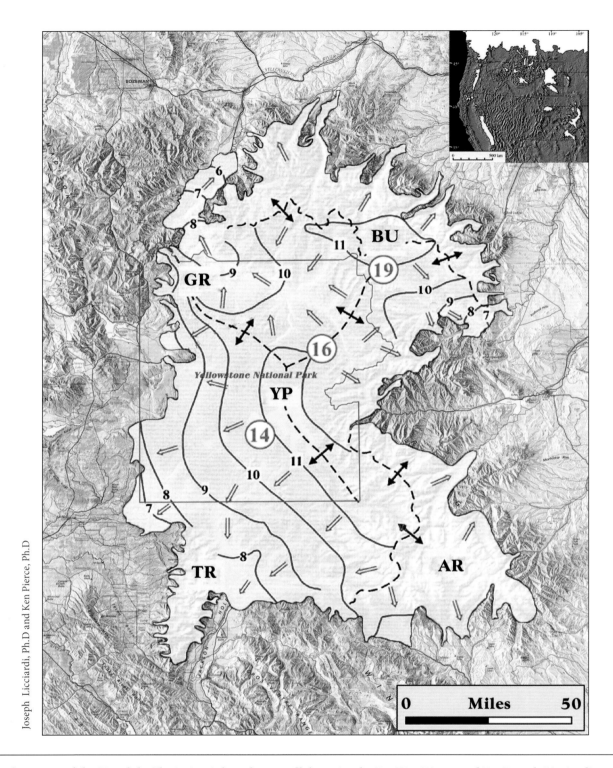

Joseph Licciardi, Ph.D and Ken Pierce, Ph.D

This depiction of the Pinedale Glaciation is based on a collaboration by Dr. Ken Pierce and Dr. Joseph Licciardi, two accomplished geologists. The irregular white expanse extending beyond Yellowstone National Park boundaries depicts the extent of the Pinedale ice. Bold black letters abbreviate key geographical points: BU for Beartooth Uplift, GR for Gallatin Range, YP for Yellowstone Plateau, TR for Teton Range, and AR for Absaroka Range. The blue contours mark the surface elevation of the glacial ice, which was generally 1,000 to 4,000 feet thick. Green numbers indicate the extent of glacial meltback in thousands of years before present. Black hash lines mark dividing ridges in the ice mass, with the black directional arrows spanning mountain divides and indicating contrasting directional flows away from the icy crests.

A computer enhanced satellite image depicts Yellowstone park as an ice filled basin just right of center. Wyoming's Wind River Mountains extend diagonally at lower right, while central Idaho's mountains are the dark mass at upper left. Montana's Yellowstone River Valley is at upper right. The large, curved Snake River Valley begins at the lower left side of the image, then arcs to the south before sweeping back to make a bull's-eye on the Yellowstone caldera.

The image illustrates how the volcanic hotspot that is presently beneath Yellowstone has been gnawing its way though the Rocky Mountains over the last 15 million years, leaving the Snake River Plain in its wake. Indeed the Snake River Valley has the serpentine appearance of an enormous subterranean monster poised to rise and take its next chomp out of the mountains to the east of Yellowstone.

This British Broadcasting Corporation image also illustrates how the Snake River Valley, with its southwest to northeast orientation, acts as a conduit to funnel Pacific moisture to Yellowstone, a phenomenon accounting for the vast amounts of ice that accumulated in Yellowstone during successive ice ages, as well as for the park's heavy winter snows in modern times.

A wickiup in a wintry setting in Yellowstone. Some of these conically-shaped, brush shelters, probably built no later than about 1880, managed to stay upright until recent times. Contemplating this photograph can conjure questions about how much time Yellowstone's aboriginal inhabitants may have spent in what is now the park during winter.

II

Yellowstone's First Peoples

"400 Generations In Yellowstone"

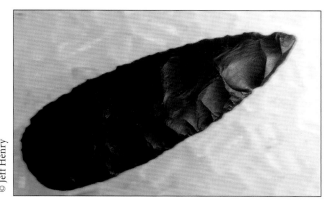

This extraordinary artifact from the Clovis culture is over 11,00 years old. It is part of a spectacular assemblage of over 100 Clovis artifacts found just north of Yellowstone National Park.

The first human beings to appear in the Yellowstone area, at least the first ones about whose presence there is no controversy, were members of the Clovis culture. They arrived in the area about 11,500 to 12,000 years ago, well after the Yellowstone Plateau had become ice free. One of the Clovis peoples' wonderfully wrought and distinctive projectile points was found in 1959 at a construction site in Gardiner, Montana, just outside the park's north boundary. The point was made from obsidian, and although the artifact was lost to science before it could definitely be linked to lithic quarries at Obsidian Cliff inside the park, it would seem likely that Obsidian Cliff was the source of its parent material. In 1968 an extraordinary find of over 100 Clovis artifacts was discovered by chance about 65 miles north of Yellowstone, near the town of Wilsall, Montana. The partial skeleton of a small child was also found with the deposit, which came to be known as the Anzick Site. In spite of the site's close proximity to Yellowstone, it is interesting to note that none of the artifacts had been made from obsidian. Near Worland, Wyoming the discovery of a Clovis point in 1962 led to archeological work at what was named the Colby Site, on the Bighorn River about 130 miles east of Yellowstone. Investigations there eventually uncovered the remains of at least seven mammoths that had been killed by Clovis hunters. Another fragment of a Clovis point was discovered in the Upper Yellowstone Valley in more recent times, but beyond these tantalizing traces, evidence of the Clovis culture in the Yellowstone region is very sparse. Still, this is enough to know that Clovis people were here and that they must have traversed what is now Yellowstone.

The Yellowstone that the Clovis people knew, although no longer covered with glacial ice, was almost certainly colder than it is today. In addition to surviving the wintry climate, these pioneering people were clever enough to fashion weapons and to devise hunting strategies adequate to kill huge herbivores, and obviously were able to do so without getting killed or seriously injured very often. They also coped with a formidable array of Pleistocene predators. They traveled or at least traded over long distances, as evidenced by the variety of stone used in their tools and weapons. They must have been impressive people, to say the least, and they must have known some form of snowshoes. But with the scanty evidence available, it is impossible to say whether the Clovis people spent any time on the Yellowstone Plateau in winter. In the commonly held image, the Pleistocene animals they hunted were well adapted to wintry climates, so possibly it can be assumed that some wildlife spent winters in the high country of what is now Yellowstone.

A possible further assumption would be that Clovis hunters also spent time on the Yellowstone plateaus

© David Joaqin

"Homeward Bound" by California artist David Joaquin depicts a Sheepeater Indian walking with his dogs down Soda Butte Creek near its junction with Lamar River. The scene is early winter, for the man is not wearing snowshoes and his dogs are dragging travois, not toboggans.

in winter to hunt those animals. Even if we accept the fact, however, that the overall climate in Clovis times was cooler and snowier than the present, there can be no question that the lower elevations around Yellowstone were less wintry in a relative sense than the high plateaus, and the most likely interpretation is that Pleistocene wildlife followed the pattern of wildlife today, where they used the high country in summer and retreated to the valleys in winter. In short, the Yellowstone plateaus probably saw little human use in the winter during late Pleistocene times.

Summer occupation of the Yellowstone Park area was more or less continuous from the time of Clovis, but even in later times there is little to no archeological evidence that native peoples used the high Yellowstone plateau country in winter. A possible exception to the seasonality of use was during the so-called Altithermal period, which began about 7,000 years ago and lasted for approximately 3,500 years. The particu-

lars of the Altithermal are much debated, but generally it is accepted that conditions in the Rocky Mountains at that time were considerably warmer and dryer than the present. In a revealing example of how things might have been in the particular case of Yellowstone, some scientists believe that conditions were so much warmer and dryer that there may have been no outflow from Yellowstone Lake. If the climate really was that much warmer and dryer, it seems reasonable to believe that ungulates would have shifted their range upward in elevation, and perhaps even spent at least portions of the winter at higher elevations. Indeed, some anthropologists believe that the Northern Plains became almost uninhabitable as a consequence of the Altithermal, and that both wildlife and human hunter/gatherers were forced to take extended refuge in the mountains. But again, there is no firm archeological evidence from the Altithermal that can tie human activity in Yellowstone to the winter season.

The Tukudikas, a branch of the Shoshone Tribe, were another possible exception to the pattern of migrating to lower elevations to avoid Yellowstone's harsh winters. At the time of white contact the Sheep-eaters, as they have been most commonly designated, lived in the mountains of northwestern Wyoming, eastern Idaho and southcentral and western Montana. A more accurate translation of the name Tukudika might be "Eaters of Meat," as their names for themselves seem to have been descriptive and to have changed frequently according to changes in primary food sources. To some extent, the Tukudika seem to have found themselves at a disadvantage as a consequence of being caught in the middle of middlemen. Neighboring tribes had access to white traders, and therefore were able to procure guns and other trade goods that gave them a competitive advantage over

tribes that did not. For obvious reasons, tribes with access to trade goods usually did all they could to deny other tribes the same access. Finding themselves surrounded by better armed tribes was an unfortunate situation for the Tukudika and other groups of Shoshone that apparently developed sometime before 1805. In that year Lewis and Clark met a branch of the Shoshone in southwestern Montana. A leader of that group named Cameahwait, who happened to be Sacagawea's brother, lamented to the captains that because his people did not have guns and ammunition they had to "...live in the mountains and live on roots and berries...." Cameahwait added that his people would have preferred to live out on the plains and hunt the buffalo that were still numerous at the time. But the nearby buffalo plains were controlled by the

"Buffalo Chase on Snow Shoes," George Catlin

An 1830s' painting from the pioneering western artist George Catlin, showed Indians using both spear and arrow to kill a bull bison mired in deep snow. Catlin painted several renditions of this composition, and explained the scene thusly: *"In the dead of winters, which are very long and severely cold in this country, where horses cannot be brought into the chase with any avail, the Indian runs upon the surface of the snow by the aid of his snow shoes, which buoy him up, while the great weight of the buffaloes, sinks them down the middle of their sides, and ... ensures them certain and easy victims to the bow and lance of their pursuers."*

While the setting for this painting is near the confluence of the Yellowstone and Missouri rivers, several hundred miles from what is now Yellowstone Park, there is abundant evidence that Indians from that area frequently traveled to the upper Yellowstone, and undoubtedly ideas were readily interchanged between native groups. An 1805 entry in Lewis and Clark journals, for example, mentions Shoshone Indians using snowshoes on their winter hunts near the headwaters of the Missouri River just west of the present park. It seems certain that the indispensable winter accessory was available to native people in the immediate Yellowstone National Park area.

much better armed and decidedly warlike Blackfeet Indians.

Thirty years after Lewis and Clark's meeting with the Shoshones, trapper Osborne Russell encountered a small band of what he called Snake Indians (the Shoshones were often called "Snakes" by the trappers because they used an undulating movement of the hand to refer to themselves in sign language) in Yellowstone's Lamar Valley. Notably, Russell did not refer to these Indians as Sheepeaters, and actually it seems that the name did not appear until much later in western history, when it may have originated with government Indian agents who were trying to bureaucratically distinguish between different groups of Shoshones.

The band Russell and his companions met was composed of six men, seven women and "8 or 10 children," and they appeared to be the "only Inhabitants of this lonely and secluded spot." At first sight of Russell and his companions the small band of Indians fled to some overlooking heights, but after realizing that the white trappers meant them no harm they descended and the two groups actually camped together for the night. Some of what the Indians told the trappers would imply that they spent the entire year within the mountains. Among other hints that this was the case was a map that the Indians drew for the trappers of the surrounding countryside with a piece of charcoal on a "white Elk Skin." The map was accurate for the surrounding mountains, and for the Lamar and Yellowstone rivers downstream from Lamar Valley to the point where the Yellowstone entered a "large plain." Significantly, the drawer of the elk hide map did not know the extent of the plain, which was "beyond his geographical knowledge or conception." If this particular band of Shoshones seasonally migrated to lower elevations at all, it seems they only went as far as the near edge of the Yellowstone Valley, at its interface with the mountains. If they actually did spend winters in Lamar Valley or in some other high elevation site in the immediate area, they must have used special survival skills to do so. Living at that high elevation and dealing with deep snow and strong cold would have increased their caloric needs in an area where sources of food were much reduced in winter. They also would have had to begin the winter with a large store of stone material, as projectile points and tools would have been lost in the snow and otherwise worn out during the course of a winter, and lithic quarries where stocks could be replenished would have been buried beneath the snow. It is worthy of note, however, that Russell described these people as "perfectly contented and happy," and although poorly outfitted with manufactured goods, "They were well armed with bows and arrows pointed with obsidian." They also had in their possession "a large number of Elk Deer and Sheep skins...of the finest quality." If this band had indeed been relegated to the mountains on a year round basis by better equipped enemies, they had done a good job of making the best of their situation.

There are a few other tantalizing clues that suggest that aboriginal Indians may have spent at least part of winter in what is now Yellowstone, at least at some times and in some places. In their excellent book *Restoring a Presence: American Indians and Yellowstone National Park*, Peter Nabokov and Lawrence Loendorf refer to the Dead Indian Creek site in Sunlight Basin just a few miles east of the park. Somewhere around 4,200 to 4,500 years ago natives camped on the site and hunted mule deer and other animals in the surrounding area between October and March, the season of the year determined by the stage of tooth development in animal skulls recovered during archeological excavations there. The site is not only near Yellowstone, it is comparable to the park in several important aspects, such as its 6,500' elevation and its general habitat type. If people were able to survive the winter at Dead Indian Creek, it seems reasonable to think that they or other people with a similar culture could have done so in the park as well.

Nabokov and Loendorf also make mention of Salish hunters from what is now western Montana who sometimes made autumn hunts in the Yellowstone area. The authors' contemporary Salish informant told them that if hunting and foraging happened to be good and sufficient stocks of food were collected, his ancestors "might stay all winter" in Yellowstone, possibly because "they liked the hot water." Presumably Indians liked soaking and bathing in warm geothermal water as much as anyone else, and an interesting sidebar is an obvious dam across a channel of a geothermal stream in the Lower Geyser Basin north of Old Faithful. The dam was constructed a very long time ago, as indicated by thick geothermal incrustations, and is considered an archeological site. The dam pools the flow of Tangled Creek, which is a runoff stream from two large hot lakes a short distance upstream and therefore comprised nearly 100% of geothermal water. The most plausible interpretation of the site is that the dam was constructed to make a wide and deep swimming or bathing pool, and one

© Jeff Henry

Replicas of a Clovis projectile point on the left and a Scottsbluff point on the right are set in a snowbank in front of a herd of frosty bison in Yellowstone's Firehole Valley. Whether or not Yellowstone's first human inhabitants spent winters in what is now the park depended on the availability of wintering ungulates more than on any other factor.

has to wonder whether the people who constructed it used the pool in the summer of the winter, or both. This latter point seems especially pertinent when one considers that the pool is filled with water that is quite warm, downright hot during the warmer months, and that it is located on a wide and open geothermal plain that is usually sunny and hot in summer. Winter would seem to be a more appealing time to soak or bathe there.

One final tidbit from Nabokov and Loendorf is an 1887 account of a few Bannock Indian families traveling through the Tower Junction area, possibly on the old Bannock Indian Trail. The account comes from some white hunters who were camped in the area and saw the Indians pass by in January of that year. Judging by the tone of the hunters' account, they were a bunch of good old boys out on some sort of male bonding bacchanal as much as they were on a hunt, and were obviously prejudiced against Indians. Furthermore, the writer makes lame attempts to inject humor into his passage by focusing on the debauchery of his fellows and the plight of the Indians, and in all the account must be taken with a grain of salt. On the Indian side it must be remembered that this was 1887, when the Indians were both culturally shell shocked and functionally desperate, so the incident might not necessarily be reflective of the way things had been in earlier days. Nonetheless, it is interesting to note that the Indians were using toboggans that were hauled by harnessed dogs and, if the account is to be believed, had enjoyed some hunting success as evidenced by the meat and hides lashed to the sleds. Conspicuous by its absence was any specific mention of snowshoes, although reasonably it would seem that the Indians must have been using them as a logical adjunct to

toboggans. Perhaps the writer did not mention them because he thought their presence was a given.

With their life ways based on hunting animals and gathering plants, it probably rarely made sense for early human inhabitants to stay the winter in Yellowstone's cold and snowy high country, especially when much lower valleys are relatively close by. Through all the history of human occupation of the area, most of the animals that spent summers in the mountains must have migrated to lower elevations outside the present park in winter, and native hunters undoubtedly followed them on their seasonal migrations. Still, in that long sweep of over 11,000 years it seems that some people must have snowshoed across the park, at least occasionally. Snowshoes were known and used by native people in the Yellowstone region, and it would seem that basic human curiosity would have been enough for at least irregular visits to the high country in winter.

Anthro Research

This fragment of an obsidian Clovis point was unearthed during construction of the Gardiner, Montana post office in 1959.

"John Colter Meets the Crows, 1807"

Western artist John Clymer painted this interpretation of John Colter's famous trek through the Yellowstone country in 1807 and 1808. The setting is along the South Fork of the Shoshone River late in the year 1807. The composition fits a popular version of the trapper's trek, which has him traveling far to the south, up the Bighorn Basin, or even through the tangle of mountains to the east and south of Yellowstone National Park, before heading west into Jackson's Hole.

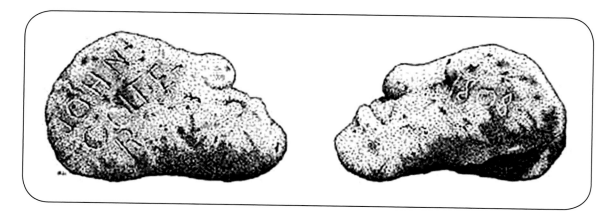

Both sides of the Colter Stone, with "John Colter" incised on one side and "1808" on the other, are shown here. The stone was plowed up by two farmers in 1931 near Tetonia, Idaho, in the Teton Valley on the west side of the Teton Range. The stone may have been engraved by Colter himself, possibly in his winter bivouac during the winter of 1807-1808.

III

John Colter

"In the Winter, on Snowshoes, Alone?"

Trail of a solitary snowshoe trek in Hayden Valley.

Famous mountain man John Colter is almost universally credited with being the first white man to visit what is now Yellowstone National Park. A veteran of the Lewis and Clark Expedition, Colter stayed in the West when the rest of the Corps of Discovery returned to Saint Louis in the autumn of 1806. In late 1807, while in the employ of fur trader Manuel Lisa, Colter was sent out on a reputed 500 mile journey to recruit Indian customers for a new trading post Lisa had built on the Yellowstone River at the mouth of the Bighorn, about 150 linear miles northeast of the present park. The favorite version of Colter's odyssey, perhaps the most popular because it is the most romantic, has the legendary trapper crossing the Yellowstone country in the winter, on snowshoes, and alone.

Students of John Colter's solitary, winter sojourn have scoured the decidedly scanty evidence of Colter's route for years and developed a popular account of his travel through Yellowstone country. However, based on early maps, topography, and the reality of what a Yellowstone winter represents, the author opines that popular accounts reflect exactly the opposite of Colter's travels during the winter of 1807-1808 and offers the following discussion.

The best available records indicate that Colter set out from the trading post at the mouth of the Bighorn, which Manuel Lisa had named Fort Raymond in hon-

or of his son, in either October or November of 1807. He traveled up one of the tributaries entering the Yellowstone River from the south, probably either the Clark's Fork of the Yellowstone River or Pryor Creek, then crossed relatively minor divides to reach the forks of the Shoshone River just west of today's Cody, Wyoming. The forks of the Shoshone, or the Stinkingwater, as the stream was known to Colter and to the mountain men who followed him in later decades, are geographically strategic. Not only do the North and South forks of the Stinkingwater come together there, the spot is also located where the main fork of the river debouches from the mountains into the Bighorn Basin. A noteworthy collection of hot springs and other geothermal phenomena, more prevalent in Colter's time than today, were also found in the immediate area. Contrary to much popular belief, these thermals around the forks of the Stinkingwater were the Colter's Hell of the mountain men, not the much larger and more numerous thermal basins in Yellowstone Park. Apparently, and there is evidence that the name was derived by translation from an Indian term for the stream, the malodorous emanations from Colter's Hell had a powerful effect on early travelers, for they were the reason for the name Stinkingwater. In actuality, the waters flowing in the river are quite pure, except when muddied by spring runoff or summer thunderstorms.

Published in 1814, Captain William Clark's map of western North America (facing page) was a prodigious achievement. Compiled from Lewis and Clark's 1804-1806 Corps of Discovery experiences, interviews with American Indians, and from information supplied by fur traders, Clark's map contributed substantially to geographic knowledge.

One of Clark's informants was John Colter, a former member of the Corps of Discovery. Colter's 1807-1808 winter route through today's Yellowstone National Park is highlighted on an enlarged portion of Clark's map (facing page, bottom). The peculiar duplication of route that Colter made in the vicinity of modern Cody, Wyoming is highlighted in light blue. A reasonable surmise is that Colter traveled back and forth on that short segment of his trek in an attempt to make contact with Indians, most likely Shoshone, who could provide him with directions, horses, or guides.

The commonly held version of Colter's trip maintains he followed his circuitous route in a clockwise manner; that is, traveling the southern loop of the route during the dead of winter. However, based on considerations involving Colter's pre-trek knowledge, topography, snow deposition and the availability of wintering wildlife, it is the author's opinion that Colter followed the counter-clockwise path, illustrated below.

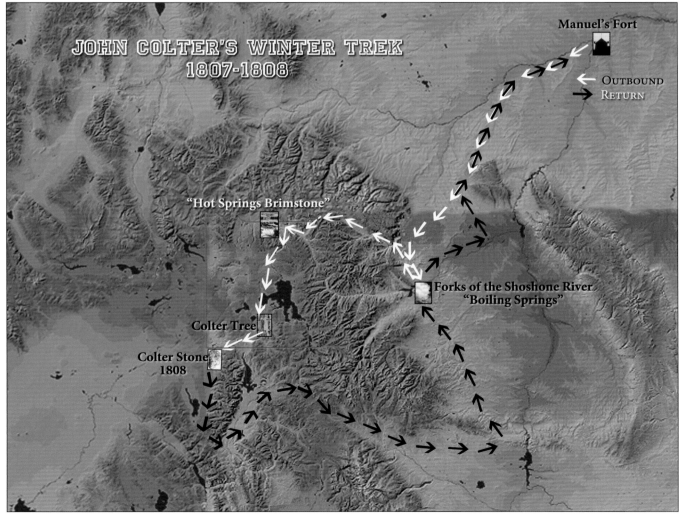

From a point somewhere in the vicinity of the forks of the Stinkingwater, Colter proceeded on a huge circle that ultimately brought him back to the same spot, but not before taking him around much of what today we call the Greater Yellowstone Ecosystem. (An interesting aside is that a careful tracing of the author's interpretation of Colter's supposed route yields a distance closer to 900 miles rather than the usually given total of 500.) Most interpreters of the intrepid explorer's trek think he began by traveling up the South Fork of the Stinkingwater. Some believe he crossed over the mountains at the head of the South Fork in a westerly direction that brought him to Jackson's Hole in the vicinity of Jackson Lake. Subscribers to this theory have probably never seen the mountains at the head of the South Fork, and have almost certainly never seen them in winter. Steep slopes grading to cliffs make such a climb treacherous in summer and, because of ice and snow, impossible in winter. If Colter did journey up the South Fork, he probably crossed out of the valley in a more southerly direction, or perhaps even retraced his steps to the vicinity of modern Cody, then turned south along the east front of the Absaroka Mountains. This seems much more probable, as this latter course eventually would have taken him to the Wind River Valley. From the upper Wind River he could have crossed into Jackson's Hole via Togwotee Pass or Union Pass, either of which would have offered a far more feasible crossing of the mountains forming the Continental Divide than the cliffs at the head of the South Fork of the Stinkingwater.

From Jackson's Hole, indications are that Colter crossed to the west side of the Teton Mountain Range via Teton Pass. A stone plowed up by some farmers on the west side of Teton Pass in 1931 had been carved into the rough shape of a human head, and engraved with "John Colter 1808." Some academicians today believe in the authenticity of the stone, that John Colter himself actually did the carving during a break on his trip. An interesting tidbit from the journals of Lewis and Clark that may give a hint of authenticity to the Colter Stone is an entry from November 18, 1805. On that date the captains were exploring the mouth of the Columbia River in search of a suitable spot to locate their winter encampment, and toward that end had asked for volunteers who "wished to See more of the Ocean." Most of the members of the Corps of Discovery were too exhausted to participate, but John Colter was one of ten who did step forward. Not only does this say something about Colter's fortitude and natural curiosity, but Captain Clark also mentioned

that when this party passed some points of land that jutted out toward the water they found some "Soft Clifts of yellow, brown & dark Soft Stones here Capt Lewis myself & Severl. Of the men marked our names day of the month & by Land &c. &c." Clark did not write specifically that Colter was one of the men who carved his name into stone, but at the very least Colter witnessed other members of his party do so. If the Colter Stone is indeed authentic, the date 1808 establishes that the new year had arrived before Colter carved the stone in the Teton Basin, which is at the approximate apex of his loop.

To continue further with the assumption that Colter walked his great loop in a clockwise direction, it appears that he traveled north along the west side of the Tetons, then recrossed that range in an easterly direction, possibly by way of Conant Pass. After crossing back to the east side of the Tetons, some evidence suggests that he traveled up the Snake River, perhaps arriving at that stream after traveling in a northerly direction down today's Coulter Creek. In 1889 some hunters along Coulter Creek found a tree near the stream about ¾ of a mile above its mouth that bore a large "X" and the initials "JC." Judging by appearances, the hunters thought the carvings to be in the range of 80 years old. The tree was later cut down by park officials, whose intention was to transport the relic to park headquarters at Mammoth Hot Springs and keep it for posterity, but there was bureaucratic bungling somewhere along the way and the section of tree trunk was lost. Modern historians generally attribute the carving to a John Coulter, who was a professional botanist accompanying an official exploration party to Yellowstone in 1872. Coulter Creek was definitely named for this latter individual during the 1872 trip, but it must be reiterated that the 1889 hunters actually saw the tree while modern historians have not. It could also be said that the hunters might have been seeing what they wanted to see when they looked at the carvings on the tree beside Coulter Creek.

The best evidence suggests that Colter's route led north from Coulter Creek to Yellowstone Lake, that he followed around the west side of the lake and then down the Yellowstone River below the lake. It appears that he crossed the Yellowstone River in the vicinity of Tower Falls, and then traveled up Lamar River and over Colter Pass on the east side of present day Cooke City, Montana. From there he traveled through Sunlight Basin, then out of the basin by way of either the Clark's Fork Canyon or Dead Indian Hill and returned to a point near the forks of the Stinkingwater, and then he retraced his outgoing route to Fort Raymond at the mouth of the Bighorn.

The best record we have for tracing Colter's route is an 1814 map drawn by Captain William Clark. Clark had a talent for map making, and he produced nearly all the maps from the celebrated Lewis and Clark Expedition of 1804-1806. Impressively, Clark kept sketch maps of the entire route of the expedition, and after his return to St. Louis he used the field sketches to begin work on a master map of what he called "the Western Portion of North America from the Mississippi to the Pacific Ocean." Clark also incorporated information he gathered from subsequent travelers to further refine his map of what would become the northwestern United States. One of these travelers was, of course, John Colter, and "Colter's Route in 1807" shows up on the 1814 final copy of Clark's handiwork. Significantly, however, there is no indication of the direction that Colter traveled as he described his great loop through the Yellowstone country.

"John Colter" by western artist E.S. Paxson.

The 1814 map is quite accurate along the route of Lewis and Clark's trip, which included the area along the Yellowstone River from a point near present day Livingston, Montana downstream to the river's mouth. Clark had begun work on his map of the Yellowstone River and its southern tributaries using detailed information he gathered from Indians in what is now North Dakota when the Corps of Discovery spent the winter of 1804-1805 at Fort Mandan. Clark himself had traveled the section of the Yellowstone below Livingston with a portion of the Corps of Discovery in the summer of 1806, and most of the later travelers to the region who furnished Clark with additional information had begun their journeys into the unknown from that river. Not surprisingly, however, the further one looks away from Lewis and Clark's traveled routes the less accurate Clark's map becomes. Nonetheless, it is possible to pick out features on the map that correspond with known elements of the landscape. The map is quite accurate along the first section of Colter's route, traveling as he did to the south up tributaries of the Yellowstone. The forks of the Shoshone, or Stinkingwater, River are well depicted, as are the thermal features near the forks. South and west of the forks details on the map become vague, with linear depictions of mountain ranges having little value beyond that of visual composition, but a body of water called Lake Biddle by Captain Clark can easily be construed as today's

Jackson Lake along the Snake River north of Jackson, Wyoming. A range of mountains shown to the west of Lake Biddle on Clark's map can be interpreted to be the Teton Range, and the tracing of Colter's route can be seen as crossing Teton Pass to the South of Lake Biddle and recrossing the same range to the north of the lake, possibly on Conant Pass. The discovery of the Colter Stone in the Teton Basin in 1931 would fit with this interpretation, as it was found along Colter's presumptive route on the west side of the Teton Range, not far from the west side of Teton Pass.

Colter's route north of the Teton area could be seen as roughly approximating the course of today's road through the South Entrance of Yellowstone National Park to Yellowstone Lake, and the Lake Eustis on Clark's map corresponds well with Yellowstone Lake. Alternatively, the route could be seen as passing to the east of today's highway along the course of Coulter Creek, which could account for the presence of the Colter Tree along Coulter Creek. The dotted line of Colter's route on Clark's map follows around the south and west sides of Lake Eustis before paralleling the Yellowstone River for a considerable distance downstream from the lake. The route is shown as crossing the Yellowstone, or the Roche Jaune as Clark often called it, at a point that could be interpreted (and often is) to be near Tower Falls. A notation on the map in Clark's hand near the depiction of Colter's crossing of the Yellowstone reads "Hot Springs Brimstone," and this is often suggested as evidence that the crossing was actually at Tower Falls, as there are a number of geothermal outlets and barren geothermal soil in the area around a ford in the river that can be feasibly crossed by a man on foot. It should be noted, however, that Indians and trappers routinely made river crossings that we see as impossible today, so the ford at Tower should not be seen as the only possible place for a man to cross on foot. This would have been especially true if Colter actually did trek through Yellowstone in winter, when many miles of the Yellowstone River are frozen solid and a man on foot could simply walk across the ice. As a matter of fact, a man on snowshoes could easily cross Yellowstone Lake on the ice, if he happened to be there in mid to late winter. From the depicted crossing of the Yellowstone, the route on Captain Clark's map traces to the east, along what could be the Lamar River Valley, although there is no representation of a stream along the route. After passing some more of Clark's linear mountains, the tracing returns to the region of the Upper Clark's Fork of the Yellowstone, where the map is again more accurate,

and from there wends off in the direction of Manuel Lisa's fort.

If John Colter traveled the route represented on William Clark's map, and there is enough evidence to make it reasonable to think that he did, it seems more likely that he traveled the route in a counterclockwise direction, or counter to the direction in most interpretations of his journey. If he traveled the great loop in a clockwise direction, as is most often suggested, he would have passed over the Yellowstone Plateau later in his journey, in the dead of winter when snow pack was at its deepest and temperatures at their lowest. It would have been especially difficult for him to ascend the Yellowstone Plateau from the south, as that part of the park is the snowiest in Yellowstone and accumulations there can reach truly awesome, and awesomely fluffy, depths. The effort required to move through such a landscape and to survive very cold temperatures would have been compounded by the almost certain absence of game animals in winter from the portion of the Yellowstone Plateau that Colter supposedly traversed. The question arises, what did Colter eat while he was trekking across Yellowstone? He is described as having carried a pack of only 30 pounds on his trip, not including things like his rifle, shot pouch, powder horn and knife that he carried on his person outside his pack. How did he carry enough food while crossing so large an area of high and wintry country where prospects for resupply were almost nonexistent? Of course, we cannot know the distribution of wintering wildlife in Colter's time. But given what is known from more recent history and from the present time, the chances of Colter encountering game animals along his purported route through the southern and eastern sides of Yellowstone simply would not have been very good.

If, on the other hand, Colter trekked in a counterclockwise direction on his great loop, he would have crossed Yellowstone in the late autumn or early winter. He is recorded as leaving Fort Raymond in October or November of 1807. If he left in the earlier portion of that time frame, he would have had ample time to cross Yellowstone—the largest block of high and snowy country on his whole route—before the onset of winter. That said, it could be further reasoned that Colter reached the site of the Colter Stone on the west side of the Teton Range before winter commenced, or perhaps just as the snow and cold were beginning to intensify. He could have made a winter bivouac there, and the stone could have been something he carved while idling away his time in

An early winter view of Yellowstone National Park's Hayden Valley presents the harsh nature of Yellowstone's high plateaus in winter. It seems unlikely that John Colter crossed this country in the dead of winter, as most interpretations assert that he did. Photographed in early winter when snow depths were still below the tops of the sagebrush, the scene is austere, with a blizzard blowing in from the hills in the distance to the west, and only a faint set of coyote tracks in the foreground indicates the presence of animal life.

camp. Lewis and Clark had formally retired to winter camp in late autumn all three winters that Colter had spent with them.

Via Yellowstone, a rough approximation of the distance from Lisa's fort to the site of the Colter Stone would be 350 miles. Even allowing for some extra miles for errors in navigation or for detours to visit Indian camps off the main route, Colter could easily have hiked that distance in say, 20 days. As a rule of thumb, the first permanent snows begin to accumulate in Yellowstone in the first week of November. Furthermore, we fortunately have an estimate of the distance Colter might have achieved on a daily basis. George Droulliard was a fellow veteran of the Lewis and Clark Expedition, and coincidentally was working for Manuel Lisa out of Fort Raymond at the same time as John Colter. Droulliard also reported what he

learned about regional geography to William Clark for incorporation onto Clark's master map. In reporting his travels to Clark, Droulliard used a figure of 30 miles per day to estimate the distances he covered. Most of Droulliard's explorations for Lisa were on open plains country east of the Rocky Mountains where travel was easier. Even allowing for a lower daily average in the mountains along Colter's route, it seems that Colter could have covered at least half or two thirds of Droulliard's average.

Some sort of semi permanent camp in which to spend the worst of the winter season makes great sense. First of all, Colter would have reduced his energy expenditure compared to that required by continuing to slog through deep snow and exposing himself to the elements in the open. By staying in one place for a time during the depths of winter, he could have invested effort into constructing a more substantial shelter, at least more substantial than what he carried on his back for night by night use. Winters at the site of the Colter Stone, near present day Tetonia in the Teton Valley, are by no means mild, but are far less harsh and less enduring than winter on Yellowstone's much higher plateaus and mountains. There are numerous streams that flow westward out of the Tetons near the site of the Colter Stone, and their east-west orientation exposes a south-facing slope on the north side of each stream. South facing slopes offer feasible winter range for ungulates in this part of the world, so there might have been game nearby for Colter to hunt.

Gregg Losinski, a modern day wildlife biologist for Idaho Fish and Game and whose district includes the Teton Basin, relates that the basin nowadays holds mule deer and elk in the winter, and he believes both species would have been there in Colter's time as well. Gregg adds that beaver, waterfowl and fish also would have been possible sources of sustenance for Colter, the latter possibilities to be found on stream sections kept free of ice by inflowing springs. The author's own observations over the last 35 years corroborate Losinski's information, and a further point is that there is written evidence that the Teton Basin's first permanent settlers, who arrived in the area in the 1870s, were able to hunt successfully during the winter.

From the Teton Valley Colter could have seen the notch at the southern end of the Teton Range that indicates Teton Pass. While a steep and difficult climb made dangerous by the possibilities of a fall or an avalanche, the route would have been obvious and the distance to Jackson's Hole on the east side of the range comparatively short. Once in Jackson's Hole he again would have been at a comparatively low elevation with a chance for game. Similarly, crossing out of Jackson's Hole via either Togwotee Pass or Union Pass would have meant a relatively short passage through snow country before arriving in the Wind River Valley on the east side of the mountains. And if one assumes that Colter did hole up in the Teton Basin for the worst of the winter, and that he did travel his great loop in a counterclockwise direction, then his crossings of Teton and either Union or Togwotee passes would have been made in late winter or early spring, when consolidated late season snow would have further facilitated his travel across those relatively short expanses of snow country. From the Wind River Valley back to the forks of the Stinkingwater and ultimately to Fort Raymond would all have been in the chinook belt east of the mountains, where greatly reduced snow cover and the presence of game animals were near certainties.

One more point must be made about John Colter's trek through Yellowstone. As improbable as it is that he made the trip in the heart of winter, it is even more improbable that he made the trip without the help of Indian information, and more likely the accompaniment of an Indian guide or guides. No matter how capable or hardy Colter was, it would seem impossible for him to have found his way through such a tangle of mountains without local help. Even considering the probability of Indian direction, Colter's trek stands as such a bold feat of individualism that it probably is beyond the full comprehension of anyone alive today.

"John Colter, Discoverer of Yellowstone Park," E.S. Paxson's drawing of John Colter striking a bold pose on the North Rim of the Grand Canyon of the Yellowstone River illustrated Enos Mills 1917 book, "Your National Parks." The image served as the basis for this colorized version (facing page) which portrays Colter traversing present-day Yellowstone National Park in the late autumn of 1807, before much snow had accumulated.

"Roche Jaune," a superbly rendered creation by contemporary western artist Gary Carter of West Yellowstone, Montana, depicts a classic mountain man riding along the rim of the Grand Canyon of the Yellowstone River, or the "Roche Jaune" in the French vernacular of the Fur Trade Era.

IV

The Mountain Men

"Bold, Rapacious Pathfinders"

A beaver lodge in Yellowstone National Park's Bechler Meadows, early winter.

In the decades following John Colter's explorations hundreds of other mountain men visited Yellowstone. Imbuing them as we do with qualities of independence, freedom, courage, toughness, the archetype is a fundamental icon of the region, and elements of the mountain man have segued into all other outdoor figures in the mythology of the American West. Although Colter is distinguished as being the first to cross the region, in another sense he was nothing but the first. The trappers who followed so quickly and in such growing numbers behind Colter were only the leading edge of a tidal wave of white encroachment that in retrospect enveloped the West with astonishing rapidity.

One of the first developments in the wake of Colter's epic 1807-08 winter trek through Yellowstone was the establishment of another fur post at the Three Forks of the Missouri, where the Jefferson, Madison and Gallatin rivers unite to form the Missouri. The river junction is only 60 miles northwest of Yellowstone, and both the Madison and the Gallatin head in what is now the park. Built in the spring of 1810, the construction and the operation of the fort was a joint endeavor between Pierre Menard and Andrew Henry, both prominent figures in the fur trading business of the time (Menard and Henry were the field leaders for a consortium of fur capitalists which included Manuel Lisa). Not that surprisingly, Menard and Henry had managed to hire both John Colter and George Droulliard to work at their Three Forks post, and Droulliard

was doomed to die there, at the hands of the Blackfeet Indians.

In a letter written in the time leading up to the establishment of the Three Forks post to a business associate back in Illinois, Menard made an intriguing reference to two different groups of trappers who, sometime previous to the writing of the letter, had begun trapping around the Three Forks of the Missouri, then worked their way south to what he called the "Spanish River," which in the parlance of the day meant the Green River. The Green River heads in the southern extremity of the Yellowstone ecosystem. In crossing the divides between the Madison River and the "Spanish River" (as Menard's letter says the trapping parties did), the trappers might have passed through what is now Yellowstone Park.

Another letter, this one written at the Three Forks in the spring of 1810 and sent to Meriwether Lewis by his brother Reuben (who had spent the winter in the mountains and was not aware of his brother's death the previous October), records two men named Peter Weizer and Baptiste Shamplaine as having made a similar foray to the south by going up the Madison River and over a divide to the "waters of the Spanish River." Weizer was another alumnus of Lewis and Clark, and another to be employed in the early fur trade of the Rockies. Notably, a "Wiser's River" appears as a fork of the upper Snake River in today's southeastern Idaho on William Clark's 1814 map [see Chapter 3], so it seems there probably was something to the Weizer-Shamplaine trip, and that the name was applied to the river as a result of a conversation Weizer had sometime later with Clark. It definitely seems that many of the early explorers were often confused about the distinction between the Snake River system leading to the Pacific Ocean and the Green/Colorado system leading to the Gulf of Mexico, but again Weizer and Shamplaine's travels may have taken them through Yellowstone.

The Menard/Henry post at the Three Forks of the Missouri River was ill fated from the start, with grizzly bears and Blackfeet Indians harassing and killing so many of the white trappers that the fort was abandoned sometime before the autumn of 1810. The famed John Colter was one of the first to leave, when after yet another close call in a career defined by close calls he left the mountains and floated down the Missouri River to settle down on the Missouri frontier. The formidable George Droulliard was then killed and horribly mangled by the ferocious Blackfeet, which really was the final straw leading to the abandonment of the post. Pierre Menard led the larger detachment from the fort in a retreat over Bozeman Pass and back east by way of the Yellowstone Valley, north of today's Yellowstone Park.

Andrew Henry, meanwhile, led a smaller contingent up the Madison River and over the divide to the headwaters of a principal branch of the Snake River, which has been know ever since as Henry's Fork (it is another name that shows up on Clark's master map of 1814). After building some cabins to serve as winter quarters, Henry's men spent a hungry winter, surviving mostly on meat they butchered from their own horses. Nonetheless, there is evidence that the men did trap extensively during that winter, and shortly after that difficult time, several of the members of that party displayed detailed knowledge of the area south and west of today's Yellowstone that could only have been gained during their stay at Henry's Fort, as it was called, or perhaps from discussing the area with others who had explored the area previously.

Henry's Fort was situated near modern day St. Anthony, Idaho, only about 30 miles southwest of today's Yellowstone National Park. Also worthy of note is that the fort was located near the Henry's Fork of the Snake River. There are several sizeable streams that emanate from the Park's southwestern corner and fall in as tributaries to the Henry's Fork near the site of Henry's Fort. Speculative though it might be in lieu of any record, it seems reasonable to think that some of Henry's men may have entered what is now the Park on their beaver hunting forays. If they used snowshoes, they might have even made short ventures into the park in winter. Snowshoes would have necessary for winter travel in that area, for that part of the Park — usually referred to as the Bechler area — is the snowiest corner of Yellowstone.

Whether Henry's men entered what is now Yellowstone on their winter trapping forays is unknown, but it is apparent that morale and discipline were so low at Fort Henry that the troop disintegrated into smaller groups of men going separate ways by the spring of 1811. Over the next few years several of these men were destined to travel back and forth over large expanses of what was to become the northwestern United States, as their knowledge made them valuable as guides to various fur trapping and trading expeditions. Some of these expeditions moved through the Yellowstone region, especially through the Jackson's Hole area to the south, and some of the companies, or portions thereof, spent time trapping in the area.

One of the most significant of the groups to pass through Jackson's Hole was a party in the employ of fur baron John Jacob Astor, who is often distinguished in American history books as having been the first multi millionaire in the United States. In late May of 1811 the group, led by Wilson Price Hunt, had been en route to build a fur trading post at the mouth of the Columbia River on the Pacific Coast when they chanced upon three men named John Hoback, John

Two masterful compositions by noted western artist John Clymer (facing page) depict two pair of trappers operating in high and snowy environments in the dead of winter. Because of the amount of snow present, the forest type and topography in "Trappers Tree" (top) and "Winter Camp" (bottom), the scenes are highly suggestive of the upper Snake River country in northern Jackson's Hole or in the southern reaches of Yellowstone National Park. Clymer had a penchant for painting scenes from the very earliest history of white men in the American West, and he had a particular interest in the experiences of the fur trading Astorians. The two scenes pictured here may very well depict the four Astorians who stayed to trap in Jackson's Hole during the winter of 1811-1812. Clymer lived in Jackson, Wyoming during the last years of his life. He died in 1989, and unfortunately no records of what the painter had in mind when he painted "Trappers Tree" and "Winter Camp" could be found.

"Trappers Tree," Clymer Museum of Art, Ellensburg, Washington

"Winter Camp," Clymer Museum of Art, Ellensburg, Washington

Robinson, and Jacob Reznor on the Missouri River in what is today Nebraska. The latter three men had spent the previous winter with Andrew Henry at his wretched post on the Henry's Fork in the Teton Basin, and were floating down the Missouri on their way back to the United States after Henry's party had fragmented earlier that spring. Hunt persuaded Hoback, Robinson and Reznor to reverse direction and use their knowledge of the Rocky Mountains to guide

him and his rather large force on their journey to the Pacific. The three men agreed to do so and led the Astorians, as they were called, back along the trail they had just followed after fleeing Henry's post, a route that took them through Jackson's Hole just south of present day Yellowstone National Park.

After descending the Hoback River to its junction with the Snake River at the southern end of Jackson's Hole, the Astorians were impressed by "these upper

ander Carson, Louis St. Michel, Pierre Detaye, and Pierre Delaunay. (Just the sounds of those names ring with connotations of the time period as well as with the strong French flavor of the fur trade, and combine to add romance to the story.) Carson, St. Michel, Detaye and Delaunay spent the winter in the area of Jackson's Hole, and it is not much of a stretch to think that their trapping of the "upper Mad River and its neighboring streams" may have taken them into Yellowstone, especially when one considers that the Snake River and several of its tributaries arise in the park, and that the background of the French trappers probably included a traditional use of snowshoes. To give a further sense of the time and place, it should be related that the four trappers did make a good catch in Jackson's Hole during that winter of 1811-12, but while they were hauling out their furs in the spring they were attacked by Indians near the Three Forks of the Missouri River and Detaye was killed.

There were other fur companies that originated out of British Canada and made it as far south as the Yellowstone area (and even farther), and with so many known groups coming and going it would seem almost certain that some entered what is now Yellowstone National Park. At least two tantalizing references have survived from British sources that seem to indicate possible presence in the Park during the winter. One is from Donald McKenzie of the Northwest Company who, when writing about the winter of 1818-19, noted that his company trapped "in the country lying between the great south branch and the Spanish waters." The "great south branch" would be the Snake River, with the "Spanish waters" being more indeterminate but probably some fork of the

streams [which] abound in beaver, and had as yet been unmolested by the white trapper... numerous signs of beaver met with during the recent search...gave evidence that the neighborhood was a good trapping ground." Trapping prospects seemed so promising that four men were split off from the party to stay in the area and "trap upon the upper part of the Mad River [as the Snake River was then called], and upon the neighboring streams." These four men were Alex-

Colorado River, or possibly a tributary of the Great Salt Lake.

McKenzie continued by writing "I left my people... [and] taking a circuitous route along the foot of the Rocky Mountains, a country extremely dreary during a winter voyage, I reached the head water of the great south branch." McKenzie included an unmistakable description of the Tetons along the course of the headwaters of the "great south branch," so we can identify that stream with certainty as the Snake. The question would be what McKenzie considered to be the "head water" of the stream. In a relative sense, the portion of the Snake around the Tetons could be considered the headwaters of the stream, especially considering that most of McKenzie's experience had been much further downstream on the Snake, near its junction with the Columbia. More literally, the ultimate headwaters of the Snake are located inside today's Yellowstone, so perhaps Donald McKenzie did slog all the way up the Snake into what is now the Park early in the year 1819.

A bit later in history, in April of 1824, there is another vague reference from a different British fur outfit, this one the vast Hudson Bay Company. The report is from Alexander Ross, a brigade leader who recorded "Saturday 24th---we crossed beyond the Boiling Fountains. The snow is knee-deep half the people are snowblind from sun glare." Considering the context, it seems that Ross was referring to the great geyser basins on the west side of the Yellowstone National Park, although we can't know that for certain. What is really intriguing in this passage is the way he refers to "the Boiling Fountains" in a way that could be interpreted to mean that the features had been known for some time and that he used them as a landmark point of reference which he expected others to understand. Additionally, it is important to keep in mind that these are just tidbits of information from records that have survived and they say nothing about other groups that almost undoubtedly passed this way, but about whom no information has survived.

It seems very likely, for example, that Peter Weizer and Baptiste Shamplaine (sometimes spelled Champlain) traveled up the Madison River Valley from the Three Forks of the Missouri to the upper Snake River. Written accounts as well as information on William Clark's 1814 map would indicate that they did. The first logical crossing between the Madison and the Snake is Raynolds Pass, only about four or five days hiking from the Three Forks. Travel time on a horse would be even less, and from Raynolds Pass to today's Yellowstone would be only another day or so of hiking or riding, whereas just two more days travel from Raynolds Pass would have put Weizer and Shamplaine in the great geyser basins of the Firehole River. Only a few years before, Weizer had spent three long seasons traveling across the continent and back with Lewis and Clark, with each of those travel seasons amounting to something on the order of seven to nine months. A couple more days travel wouldn't have been much for Weizer, and it would seem natural for a beaver hunter to search a stream as rich in fur as the Madison to its ultimate source. And simple curiosity about the source of such a fundamental river could possibly have been enough for an explorer such as Weizer to follow the Madison as far as he could. This is not to say that Weizer and Shamplaine or any of the other fur men of their time did enter Yellowstone, but rather it is intended to point out that they easily could have. There is no mention in the extant records that they did, but it is also true that many of the people involved in the trade were illiterate, and that the conditions in which the beaver hunters lived were not conducive either to keeping or to preserving records. Whether any of the groups were in Yellowstone during the winter season is even more problematic.

The flurry of fur trading activity in the northern Rockies that followed in the wake of Lewis and Clark lasted less than ten years. It wound down largely as a consequence of the War of 1812, which restricted trade with Europe, the market for most of North America's furs, and posed a direct danger of confrontation with British elements for Americans operating in the Northwest. A period of retrenchment for American fur interests followed, during which time the fur trade focused on areas east of the Rockies and closer to bases of supply in St. Louis. The hiatus in the Rockies ended in 1822, however, when entrepreneurs in the East organized new expeditions to travel to the Far West. The next two decades saw the heyday of the fur trade in the Rocky Mountains, the time of the storied fur trading rendezvous and generally the classic period we think of when we think of mountain men. Almost uncountable fur brigades passed through Yellowstone during this time, and those are just the ones we know about. Written descriptions of most of the major features we know today in Yellowstone have survived from the 1820s and 1830s, but again there is no record of a group or of an individual spending a winter in what is now the Park. That said, there is an uncorroborated account of an army officer stating that he had been given a description of the Park's geyser basins in winter by none other than the most famous mountain man of all, Jim Bridger. The army officer, Lieutenant Frederick Schwatka, would himself lead a winter exploration party into Yellowstone in the winter of 1886-1887, but he did not relate the Bridger story until well after the trapper's death in 1881.

There are places in Yellowstone, mostly on the west side of the present park (and mostly removed from John Colter's purported route through the eastern and southern portions of the Park), where geothermal heat maintains snow free conditions and free flowing streams in even the coldest of winters. Some of these places form viable niches for wintering wildlife, as an early surveyor of Yellowstone's wintering wildlife named Elwood Thomas Hofer recorded in 1887. He noted a family of beavers near Obsidian Cliff and as many as 20 more living in a small tributary (probably Pipeline Creek) of the Firehole River near Old Faithful. Hofer predicted that the colony of 20 beavers near Old Faithful would soon restock the Firehole, indicat-ing that at least he thought the larger stream would also support the animals.

Since it is a characteristic of nature that if a niche exists it will be filled, it is likely that at least to some extent these niches were occupied even in the days before settlement of the surrounding region confined wildlife within the Park. Some trappers may have discovered this phenomenon, possibly by observing conditions after an autumn snow storm, possibly after having been delayed in what is now the park by an accident or injury that occurred in the fall of the year. All the elements necessary for a trapper or a small group of trappers to spend a winter were there — snow free ground on which to camp and where their stock animals could forage; wintering ungulates to feed the trappers; and open water where trapping could go on through the winter. Add to this the trappers' frequent desire to operate in secrecy, and it's not hard to imagine that an individual trapper or a small group spent a winter or winters in what is now the Park. As with the wildlife itself, if a niche for the trappers existed it was apt to be filled.

Andrew Langford • National Park Service

Yellowstone Gateway Museum

Jim Bridger, arguably the most famous and accomplished mountain man of all, is pictured here in his later years. An uncorroborated account from the late Nineteenth Century claimed that Bridger had spent time in Yellowstone in the winter.

V

The Prospectors

"Mineral Seeking Explorers"

Panning for gold in a Yellowstone area stream.

© Jeff Henry

Prospectors came to the Yellowstone country in the 1860s. The prospectors, who were mainly looking for gold, arrived in the area as part of a progression that began at Sutter's Mill in California in 1848. In the oft-repeated pattern, a new discovery of gold would be overwhelmed by hordes of eager miners who quickly exhausted surface deposits that could easily be recovered with simple hand tools. A few lucky or ruthless individuals would be left in possession of the bulk of the wealth produced by a strike, while the majority of the fortune seekers would be forced either to look for other occupations or to move on in search of new mineral prospects. Following the strikes in California, prospectors found other gold deposits in Oregon, Idaho, and western Montana in a sequence that resulted in significant numbers of miners operating in the region around Yellowstone by the early 1860s.

Artist Todd Fredericksen of Gardiner, Montana skillfully illustrates the author's contention that prospectors of the 1860s and 1870s may well have wintered in Yellowstone Park's geyser basins (facing page). Despite the low probability of finding gold, few streams were overlooked, and it is likely some gold seekers recognized the potential for "wintering" in the secluded, game-rich, thermally-heated geyser basins within easy, springtime striking distance of the reported gold discoveries to the east.

Overflow from Montana gold towns like Bannack, Virginia City, Nevada City and Alder Gulch led to known prospecting expeditions passing through what is now Yellowstone beginning in 1863 and continuing every year for the rest of the decade. As with the mountain men, there is the near certainty that there were other expeditions for which no records have survived. For the most part, the gold seekers followed the same topographically directed trails that the trappers had traveled a few decades earlier, searching for fortunes in gold along the same streams where the trappers had sought fortunes in furs. The prospectors added to the geographical knowledge of the area, and naturally added a number of permanent place names to the map.

With the greater national population by the time of the prospecting era, and especially because of the settlement of the surrounding region, the prospectors had a much more ready forum for their reports about the wonders of Yellowstone. It is interesting to note that reports of mineral discoveries were readily received when prospectors returning from their forays related what they had discovered. This was true in the mining settlements near Yellowstone and also for the nation as a whole, as exemplified by the fact that disaffected Confederates from the southeastern United States made up a goodly proportion of the miners in the Montana fields, and by extension the prospecting explorers of what was soon to become Yellowstone National Park.

Information regarding travel routes was also quickly absorbed and utilized, but notably reports about Yellowstone's geothermal phenomena seems to have been largely overlooked or ignored, at least until the end of the decade. Whether this was because attention was so single-mindedly focused on mineral wealth or simply because the general public wasn't ready for Yellowstone's geothermals to be discovered, the topic seems to have received surprisingly little attention in the press at the time. Given a few moments' thought, this point might have intriguing throwback implications to what the earlier mountain men might have seen and reported. National population was much lower and more remote from Yellowstone in the time of the trappers, and attention was devoted to the fur trade and to sorting out the broad geographical outlines of the West. This, coupled with the fact that people were presumably less sophisticated and communication networks more primitive, it seems even more believable that more mountain men saw Yellowstone's geothermal wonders and perhaps even reported on what they saw more frequently than we can know from the information that was published in their time.

By the end of the prospecting era miners had brought about the construction of several permanent towns quite close to Yellowstone. Some of these towns had been built directly on the site of mineral strikes, while other communities had sprung up to supply provisions to the miners and their operations. Bozeman, Montana was the most significant of the latter type. Equally important were the military posts that were established for the protection of the mining communities. Both the towns and the military installations were about to serve as supply bases and jumping off points for the official exploration of area of what soon would be designated Yellowstone National Park. In a general sense, prospecting and mining activities were just pro tempore manifestations of the Euro American juggernaut that was surging westward in the years during and especially after the Civil War. In a more specific sense, new transportation routes were established into the Yellowstone region, while older routes were improved to carry greatly increased traffic. And even before the end of the prospecting phase white people had settled near and even within what is now Yellowstone Park. Certainly by the winter of 1870-71, if not before, miners were spending the winter near today's Cooke City, Montana, just outside Yellowstone Park's present Northeast Entrance, and almost certainly were traveling back and forth across the park's northern range during the winter months.

As for winter occupation of the park itself, it seems unlikely since gold prospecting of the day was dependent on open water for washing gold out of placer deposits, and most streams in the mineralized portions of the park freeze solid during the winter. Of course there is always the possibility that some unknown group of prospectors got stuck in the park by an unexpectedly early onset of winter, or that an individual with hermit-like tendencies intentionally decided to hole up in some out of the way place in the high country of what is now the park. Indeed, there is at least one reference in the journal of an official Yellowstone explorer who had knowledge of two white men who spent the winter in what is now the park. On September 5, 1870, Lieutenant Gustavus Doane noted that the "basin [of Yellowstone Lake] would not be a desirable place for winter residence. The only two men I have been able to find who ever wintered there both came out affected with goitres [sic] in the spring."

Given the timing of Doane's presence on the Yellowstone scene, it is most likely the two individuals to whom he referred were operating as prospectors when they apparently wintered over near Yellowstone Lake. Unfortunately, Doane left us no further details about the two men, such as who they were, why they chose to spend the winter near Yellowstone Lake, and exactly where they might have camped within the lake's basin. In other writings, however, Doane did add some tantalizing details that seem to indicate that he had a fairly extensive interview with the two men (or possibly someone else — it's not completely clear) and that they had made telling observations about winter in the park. Those tidbits include information about temperatures and snow depths, the date of freeze up for Yellowstone Lake, and a wonderful description of the Lower Falls as being adorned with "gigantic pilastors of ice." Clearly, someone had seen the wonders of Yellowstone in winter and described what he had seen to Lieutenant Doane at some time after the fact. All that said, it must be stated that there is evidence that Doane revised his field journal after he had made his early winter trip, perhaps long after his trip, so his sources may also have spent their winter in the vicinity of Yellowstone Lake at some time considerably later in history that it might seem on the surface of things.

In addition to this report from Gustavus Doane, we know that a number of prospector/miners spent the winter of 1881-1882 in the vicinity of Cooke City, Montana. Prospectors in that area had found "mineral," as they often put it, as early as the 1860s. The trouble was, from the miners' point of view, the mineralized area around Cooke City and the head of the Clark's Fork of the Yellowstone was then part of the Crow Indian Reservation, having been "set apart for the absolute and undisturbed use and occupation of the Indians [the Crows]." For the miners, that inconvenient situation lasted until April 11, 1882. The area around Cooke City, which had come to be called the "New World Mining District," had by then been whittled away from the Crow Reservation and was thrown open for prospecting claims on that date. Anticipating the opening of the district to claims, "prospectors and miners were not slow in getting into the new country. They came from all the mining camps of the country, wherever the reports of the richness of the Clark's Fork mines had penetrated. *Some prospectors had waited all winter in the mountains, ready to make locations as soon as the treaty was signed* [emphasis added]; others were stationed in Bozeman and hastened over the mountains as soon as the telegraph brought the news of the relinquishment of the Indian title. *The snow was still deep and the last twenty or thirty miles had to be made on snow shoes* [again, emphasis added]."

The last line in the above paragraph was included and emphasized because of the reference to "snow shoes," which in 1882 meant Norwegian snow shoes or what today we call the cross country skis. Cross country skis and the art of their use were the most important contributions made to Yellowstone winter history during the prospecting and mining era. There will be more about that later on.

As it was in every other mineralized area of the West, the prospecting era in the Yellowstone area was brief, for the simple reason that it didn't take that long for prospectors to scour a region and exhaust the possibilities for further surface discoveries. That fact was coupled with the illiteracy of many of the people involved and the well known tendency of prospectors to operate in secrecy. The fact of the matter is that to a great extent we have to rely on conjecture to reconstruct a lot of what went on during the period.

Old Faithful Geyser's plume dominates the winter landscape of the Upper Geyser Basin. This scene is an example of the geothermal oases which might have offered a suitable winter refuge for 19th century prospectors, as it had done for their predecessors, trappers and American Indians.

Lieutenant Frederick Schwatka's ill-fated 1887 expedition was the first official winter explorations of Yellowstone National Park. Preeminent photographer F. Jay Haynes accompanied the expedition and made this image of Schwatka's party on the Grand Loop Road near Obsidian Cliff. The concave or dished profile of the snow on the road is subtle, but unmistakable, evidence of the passage of earlier traffic on the road, with a resultant packed base under the covering of a few inches of new powder on the surface — conditions which contradict Schwatka's later claims that his party was defeated by snow so soft and deep that even the large skis of the day were inadequate to prevent a skier from foundering.

VI

Yellowstone's Government Explorers

"Official Johnny Come Latelies"

© Jeff Henry

Old Faithful eruption at winter sunrise.

A little more than 60 years after John Colter's passage through Yellowstone, exploration parties that progressively became more official began to survey the area. The David Folsom party in 1869, the Washburn Expedition of 1870, and the Hayden Survey of 1871 formally explored Yellowstone, disseminated information about the region to the nation, and directly led to the establishment of the world's first national park in March of 1872. The men who conducted these surveys were socially elite, the movers and shakers of their day, and in many respects were exceptional individuals, but their discoveries were made with the obvious irony that the trails they were following and the wonders they were witnessing had been known to earlier Euro-American travelers for decades, to say nothing of having been known to the aboriginal Indians for at least 11,000 years.

Successive official surveys in the years after the park's creation filled in more information about the area, as Yellowstone came to be known to an ever finer level of detail and more and more place names were applied to its landscape. These surveys all took place in the summer months until 1876, when Lieutenant Gustavus Doane crossed Yellowstone in early winter in the company of eight other soldiers en route to conduct a winter reconnaissance of the Snake River in northwestern Wyoming and eastern Idaho.

Doane was an experienced man who had led the military escorts that accompanied both the Washburn Expedition to Yellowstone in 1870 and the Hayden Survey in 1871. He was also a Civil War veteran and had participated in several campaigns against the Indians in Montana, including the operations against the Blackfeet in January of 1870 that culminated in the massacre of 173 members of the Heavy Runner band on the Marias River. He also had been involved in the summer 1876 campaign against the Sioux that among other events had led to the Custer debacle on the Little Bighorn. If not for the vagaries of military orders, Doane could well have been directly involved in the Custer battle, and his story would have ended right there on the Little Bighorn. The mustachioed lieutenant had made at least two additional trips to Yellowstone, one each in 1874 and 1875, and throughout his career he had often displayed a practical nature. Why he chose to cross the Yellowstone plateaus so late in the year and to float the Snake River in the dead of winter is a bit of a mystery, a mystery for which the only logical explanation would seem to be Doane's demonstrated lust for fame and glory. Fortunately for us, Doane kept a journal on his trip through Yellowstone and down the Snake River, a journal which gives us a bit of a snapshot of winter conditions at the time.

On October 25, 1876, Lieutenant Gustavus Doane and his military detail camped at the outlet of Yellowstone Lake en route to their winter exploration of the Snake River. Doane observed a glorious sunset with a simultaneous moonrise over the Absaroka Mountains to the east of the lake. He was moved to describe the scene in his journal: *"The mighty ranges of the great divide were sharply outlined in cold gleaming white. Below their ragged summits dark green forest masses filled the spaces.... A picture indescribable, unequaled and alone."* The Absaroka range, above, was photographed from the approximate location of Doane's 1876 camp about 130 years later.

Doane and his detachment of one sergeant and seven privates didn't leave their base at Fort Ellis on the outskirts of Bozeman, Montana until October 11, 1876. Initially they used a wagon with eight mules to haul much of the equipment that had been assembled for the Snake River Expedition by army quartermasters, but the wagon overturned on the rough trail in Yankee Jim Canyon along the Yellowstone River just north of the park and was reduced to ruin. From that point the soldiers were forced to pack all their supplies as well as the disassembled boat on the mules. A heavy snowstorm in the Washburn Range — a portent of things to come — as well as played out pack animals delayed them to the point that they didn't reach Yellowstone Lake until October 23. Topping out on Dunraven Pass along the route to the lake, which quite likely was a segment of the trail John Colter had followed 69 years earlier, Doane was moved to write in his journal "Beyond and at our feet now lay the

Great Basin of the Yellowstone, with its dark forests, its open spaces all wintry white, and its steam columns shooting upward in every direction. It was like coming suddenly upon the confines of the unknown, so differently did the snow landscape appear in the summertime."

Taken as he was by the scene, Doane was just one of the first to note the startling contrast between the appearance of Yellowstone in winter and the Yellowstone he had seen in summer, a contrast so striking that many seeing the park for their first time in winter experience a sense of thrilling newness almost as moving as what they felt when they saw the park for the very first time. This was something he had in common with nearly all other Yellowstone visitors to follow who, like Doane, almost universally see the park in winter after having first visited it in summer. Also like many others since Doane's time, he went on to note that he "noticed no variation in the thermal spring action which might be traced to change of temperature of the atmosphere," with the exception of a greater "show of vapor."

Beginning on October 23, the expedition camped on the north shore of Yellowstone Lake near its outlet, where they spent four nights and three days organizing themselves, collecting lame stock that had been abandoned along their back trail, and reassembling their boat. Some of this latter work was done at night by candle and firelight. They used snow to moisten and make pliable their boat's planking, and collected pine pitch from the nearby coniferous forests to caulk gaps. One night, Doane straightened up from his work at preparing the boat to take further notice of the wintry scene by the light of a full moon, and wrote that peaks of the Absaroka Range on the east side of the lake "were sharply outlined in cold gleaming white," and again noted that steam columns from geothermals around the lake were more apparent in the cold air. In all he recounted the frigid scene to be "A picture indescribable, unequalled and alone....a night and a scene to be remembered — a touch of nature vibrating into infinity."

On the morning of October 27, Doane and his men began working their boat along the shore of the lake toward West Thumb, which they accomplished by using a mule on shore to tow the craft while a man on board used a pole to fend off from the beach. Although they ominously had to leave a broken down mule at their camp by the lake outlet, for a time things went fairly well, the towing mule progressing down the gravel beach at a trot and the other men with the horses and mules following along. By so doing, the expedition was quite likely taking advantage of a phenomenon often seen around Yellowstone Lake in the early winter, when relative warmth from the lake melts the snow from a belt of beach a short distance back from the water's edge, in this case leaving a snow free ribbon where the mule could travel. At midday, however, a rocky point of land forced them to unhook their towline, and two men were obliged to row the boat around the steep bluff (probably Rock Point). As the rowers rounded the point they were hit by heavy waves, which swamped the boat immediately. The water fortunately was shallow, so all the baggage from the boat was saved, but the soldiers had to build circular fires around the soaked equipment to dry it out. Not only that, but the rough water had knocked loose some of the boat's caulking, and that had to be replaced.

While waiting for things to dry and for his boat to be repaired Lieutenant Doane had time to look at the

National Park Service

Lieutenant Gustavus Cheney Doane at about the time of his Yellowstone explorations.

high country south of Yellowstone Lake, ridges forming the Continental Divide which he had to cross to access the headwaters of the Snake River, and to feel daunted by the heavy snows he could see there. As a consequence of his concern, Doane decided to divide his command, leaving three men to finish repairs to the boat while he and the others loaded the bulk of their baggage on their pack animals and forged ahead. His plan was for the horse and mule party to pack the gear over the Continental Divide to Heart Lake, one of the ultimate sources of the Snake, and then return for the boat and its three attendants. The boat then could be skidded by mules over the trail that had been broken between Yellowstone Lake and Heart Lake, where the expedition could relaunch for its exploratory float down the river. After repairing the boat, the three boatmen were to pilot the vessel across the West Thumb of Yellowstone Lake and meet the returning stock party on the south shore.

The stock party effected their crossing of the Continental Divide between the two lakes on October 29, although they had to trudge through two feet of snow and a "heavy and blinding snowstorm" to do so.

Yellowstone Lake during late autumn freeze-up. The lake was in a somewhat similar condition when Lieutenant Doane and his detail crossed it with their prefabricated boat in late October of 1876.

On the shore of West Thumb that evening Doane sent some men with the horses and mules to the West Thumb Geyser Basin so that the animals could graze on the geothermal heated and snow-free ground there. Meanwhile, on a small lakeside bluff probably near today's Grant Village, the lieutenant and at least one other man built a large signal fire for the boatmen to see. Anxiety was high, as Doane had expected the boat to arrive at the meeting place before he returned from Heart Lake and worse, as evening descended a gale developed that blew freezing sleet before it, a sleet that "adhered to whatever it touched." Doane realized that the tempest was blowing at a right angle to the course the boatmen would have to follow in their crossing of West Thumb. This means the storm was blowing in the direction of most storms in Yellowstone, that is from the southwest, and anyone who has ever boated on Yellowstone Lake knows that such storms can indeed be violent. This is especially true in the West Thumb and in its connecting channel, both of which are configured in perfect alignment with the prevailing winds.

After hours of worrying and of tramping up and down the beach in search of the missing men, the wayward boat finally arrived. The vessel and its three pilots were in dire shape, however. Doane claimed that the oars were coated with an inch of ice, that the boat was half filled with ice from spray that had frozen before it could be baled out, and that the men themselves were completely soaked, with much of the moisture frozen to their clothes, hair and beards. Doane and other members of the shore party fed the forlorn mariners and built large fires to warm them and to dry their clothes. The combined party spent most of the next day chopping ice from the boat with axes, and also throwing hot ashes into the craft to complete the job. They then fitted the bottom of the boat with saplings to serve as runners for the trip to Heart Lake and started on the drag in mid-afternoon, but not before one of their mules fell into a mud pot and scalded his lower extremities. Doane had the scalded mule led to the lake, where he figured immersion in the cold water cured the animal of his injuries.

The drag over the Continental Divide to Heart Lake took four days and "was telling on the mules on account of the depth of the snow." The endeavor required "severe labor" from the men as well, and worse yet was that the planking of the boat had shrunk and cracks had opened along all its joints, an occurrence Doane attributed to the severe cold. Rechinking the cracks first required heating the boat over a bed of low burning coals to thoroughly dry it out, and then

so. Furthermore, Doane reckoned the temperature to be well below zero by the time they reached Heart Lake late in the day. The crossing of the Great Divide in such conditions had worn out both men and stock, and the men spent most of the night huddled next to a fire to dry out, so they probably didn't get much quality rest. On a more positive note, however, Doane and his men did see a herd of elk near the Heart Lake Geyser Basin, which must have made them feel hopeful for prospects of restocking their larder, and also noticed that there was good grass in the vicinity for their horses and mules. They returned to Yellowstone Lake the next day, but by a somewhat different route, as there had been so much fallen timber on their route of the 29th that they thought it would be difficult to skid their boat that way.

caulking with pitch laboriously collected from conifers by wading through the deep snow. Finally they split long strips from green lodgepole pine saplings which they attached to the bottom of the boat so that it would slide over rocks in shallow water without damaging the vessel's integrity. Notwithstanding the elk they had seen when they first arrived at Heart Lake, the only meat they were able to harvest during their stay there was a young porcupine and possibly a duck. Lieutenant Doane spent some of this time walking around the south end of the lake in an unsuccessful search for its outlet.

Even before Doane's men completed the haul of their boat from Yellowstone Lake, the lieutenant had dispatched two privates back toward Fort Ellis with some of the pack animals. The stock sent back were considered surplus, as from this point on it was thought that the trip would be a simple downriver float and only a few horses and mules in support would be necessary. This left the ongoing expedition with seven horses and four mules, or eight less than they had when they started their trip on October 11. The two privates sent back to Fort Ellis were charged not only with returning the surplus stock to their base, but also with picking up equipment cached and broken down stock abandoned on the outgoing trip. The trip back was a "severe experience," and because the season was a bit more advanced, it gives us an even better glimpse of winter conditions in Yellowstone Park at the time. Apparently, the severe experience didn't commence immediately, as the two men felt comfortable in taking a 40 mile detour from Hayden Valley to the Firehole geyser basins, but in the basins they were beset with a major snowstorm that marooned them for two days, during which time they luckily were able to kill two elk. Returning the 40 miles to Canyon, probably via Nez Percé Creek and Mary Mountain, the two men climbed through deep snow over Dunraven Pass, where an avalanche fatally swept two of their pack mules down into Tower Creek. The two mules were loaded with the soldiers' bedding, and that loss coupled with intensifying cold weather prevented the men from sleeping at night. Because they couldn't sleep the men pushed on without many rest stops and overtaxed their remaining stock, and as a consequence arrived at Mammoth with only their two riding horses and one pack mule left. From Mammoth back to Fort Ellis their route took them through country much lower in elevation and less wintry than the park, and they arrived back at the fort "much fatigued but uninjured."

Meanwhile, Doane and the main body of the expedition finished their latest round of repairs to the boat and launched it to cross Heart Lake on November 6. The weather was bitterly cold for the crossing, with the temperature still below zero at midday, and well before reaching the outlet of the lake they encountered a snow covered expanse of ice. The ice proved solid enough for the men to bring out a pair of mules, which they used to drag the boat across the ice to the outlet of the lake and into the Heart River. The outflow from the lake was disappointingly small, however, far too little to allow their boat to float, and the men were forced to drag the craft over barely submerged rocks, often slipping and falling for want of traction on the icy stream bed. They had to unload their baggage from the boat and repack it on their remaining stock, and they sometimes used one mule to help pull the boat, but the arduous work and the lack of forage due to snow cover quickly began to tell on all the animals — within two days of accessing the Heart River they had been forced to leave behind one horse and one mule. By the third day it had snowed some more, they had worn a hole in the bottom of their boat, and the temperature was down to 20 below zero. It finally got so cold that they were able to patch holes in their boat by pouring water from a cup into the cracks. The water froze immediately into ice-caulk which held until they passed some hot springs near today's South Entrance, where warm water inflow melted the plugs and the men were obliged to lay over again for another round of major repairs. By that point, at least, the Snake had collected enough water from tributaries to enable the men to float their boat without having to wrestle it over rocks and gravel.

By November 21 the latest round of repairs had been effected — following the usual routine of drying the boat over smoldering embers and collecting sap for caulking from conifers, and of course doing all of the work in deep snow with more of it falling much of the time. This time, however, damage to the craft was so great that the men had to tear out seats and other structures from the interior of the boat and use that lumber to replace splintered planks on the bottom and sides. Those repairs completed, the group left Yellowstone Park and floated off down the Snake toward further and even more serious misadventures, some of which were nearly fatal.

Aside from nearly drowning and freezing to death, the explorers probably would have starved had it not been for the help they received in turn from a lone trapper in Jackson's Hole and from some miners in eastern Idaho. As it was, they were forced to eat one of their own horses, the flesh of which tasted "exactly as the perspiration of the animal smells." They also ate an otter, which they found fishy and which their stomachs would not tolerate, and a mule deer of questionable condition which they also blamed for making them sick. Finally, their boat was crushed by an ice jam near present day Idaho Falls, and they were forced to return to their post at Fort Ellis in January of 1877, having navigated only a relatively small portion of their intended route down the Snake and Columbia rivers.

Aside from Doane's obsessive devotion to making a name for himself, the Snake River Expedition does tell us something about winter in the park at an early day. While only one winter, the expedition's records do seem to point to the season being more severe than it is today, and especially one that sets in at an earlier date than it has in most years during the more recent past. In most of recorded history Yellowstone's winter weather, as characterized by snow on the ground that does not melt until spring and sub freezing temperatures for daily highs, has commenced sometime in early November. In more recent years, winter often has not begun until late November, whereas during Doane's ill-conceived trip winter seems to have set in fully by late October. Other anecdotal evidence supports the view that the winter season used to be both colder and snowier, as well as longer in duration, than it is today. There is also a growing body of scientific information, garnered from pollen deposits in pond sediments, tree ring analysis and other clever methods, that bolsters this view.

One winter that we know for certain was exceptionally cold and snowy was that of 1886-87. Students of western history know that winter mostly because of its impact on the open range cattle industry on the Northern Plains, where savage weather demonstrated the wisdom of taking closer care of smaller herds of livestock as opposed to allowing large herds to roam over vast areas away from oversight. Snow came to the plains of Montana in November and with the exception of a few thawing west winds (known regionally as chinooks) that actually exacerbated conditions by melting the snow just enough for it to crust over when the cold returned, the brutal weather continued for months. Some 60% of Montana's cattle

were killed by starvation and exposure, and nearby Yellowstone National Park was no exception to regional conditions. By coincidence, it was this during particular winter that Yellowstone officialdom got around to exploring the park's interior in the dead of winter.

Lieutenant Frederick Schwatka was the leader of the first official party to attempt a winter exploration of the park. By late 1886 Schwatka had established a considerable reputation for himself as an arctic explorer. The Lieutenant had conducted his several arctic trips on special detail from the United States Army, but by the time he began to plan the winter trip to Yellowstone he had resigned his commission to devote all his time to well publicized explorations designed to further his own name. For the Yellowstone trip he garnered financial support from one newspaper and one magazine, which combined to fund his trip in return for exclusive stories from the adventure. Schwatka also lined up support from the Northern Pacific Railroad, that company agreeing to transport his party to the park. The Northern Pacific had a vested interest in hostelries in Yellowstone, and also wanted to increase its passenger trade, so in addition to providing transportation for the Schwatka party and its equipment the railroad sent along its company photographer, Frank J. Haynes. Finally, Schwatka had arranged for additional support from the United States Army, which in those days before the creation of the National Park Service was charged with taking care of Yellowstone. (The army contingent assigned to protect Yellowstone had just arrived the previous August, so the soldiers were still getting themselves squared away in their new duty station.)

In spite of his arctic experience, or perhaps because of it, Schwatka compiled a long list of miscalculations about winter in Yellowstone. His most serious mistakes concerned snow conditions in the park. For some reason he thought that not much snow fell here, and that the snow that did fall was dense and therefore would be hard packed underfoot. So confident was he that snow would be of little consequence on his trip, or at least would afford good footing if it was present, that he contemplated the use of dogsleds to haul his kit around the park. Even more incredibly he considered employing Crow Indians with horses to pack the equipment on his journey, although one could speculate that this latter scheme may have been a grandstand play intended to enthrall his readership. Compounding his misconceptions about Yellowstone's snow, Schwatka assembled a mountain of gear for his endeavor, far more than could be hauled by

Jerry Brekke

Flush with his reputation as an Arctic explorer, Lieutenant Frederick Schwatka was featured on an 1886 cover of "Wonderland," Northern Pacific Railroad's publication advertising Yellowstone National Park.

brute manpower. Yet another flaw in his approach was that the men he selected for the trip had little to no experience with cross country skis, which in Schwatka's time were commonly known as Norwegian snowshoes. Beginning well before 1887 and continuing until the present time, most people familiar with winter in Yellowstone agree that cross country skis are the way to go in the park's deep and fluffy snows. Many of the men on Schwatka's roster, however, appear to have been selected on criteria other than their capabilities for winter travel. Most did not have their first experience with cross country skis until the party rendezvoused in Livingston, Montana en route to Yellowstone. There they practiced with their new skis on a small hill just outside town, where they displayed such ineptitude that a newspaper reporter was moved

to write, "Unless the party makes rapid progress in the science of snowshoeing they will be found with their tour unfinished when the snow has disappeared in the spring."

The Schwatka party of 13 men left Mammoth Hot Springs on January 5, 1887. Their intention was to follow Yellowstone's main road from Mammoth through Norris to Old Faithful, and from there to travel east to Yellowstone Lake and then north to Canyon. From Canyon they would possibly return to Mammoth by passing through Norris again, or alternatively cross the Washburn Mountains to Tower and return to Mammoth that way. When the party left Mammoth they had so much gear that they had to transport some of it in an army wagon hauled by mules, but the wagon made it only as far as Swan Lake Flat, or about four or five miles out of Mammoth, where it foundered in deep snow and had to turn back. At that point the men reorganized their baggage and loaded at least some of it onto toboggans, which they towed behind them as they shuffled along on skis, but there was only enough daylight left to make it to Indian Creek, marking a total of about eight miles on their first day. That first night out the temperature, which had been unusually mild when they left Mammoth, fell to 37 degrees below zero.

On the morning of the 6th the group stashed the largest portion of their gear and supplies in a building near their campsite at Indian Creek, retaining a much reduced kit that they carried on the toboggans and on their persons. They then shuffled south on the Mammoth-Norris road, but again had great difficulty with conditions and with their own inexperience, so their net distance for the day was only two miles. They camped that night near Willow Park. The next day they did manage to make it the rest of the way to Norris, although lagging members of the group didn't arrive there until 10:00 o'clock that night, and their total for three days' effort was barely 20 miles. They holed up at Norris in the Norris Hotel, which had just been completed the previous autumn and which was being looked after by a man named Kelly, who was serving as the winterkeeper there. Winterkeeper is the term that apparently has always been used for the caretakers who shoveled snowloads from roofs and kept an eye on hotels and other properties during the off seasons in Yellowstone, especially

Sketch artist Henry P. Bosse, pictured here at Norris Geyser Basin in mid-January 1887, accompanied the Schwatka party on its truncated winter exploration in Yellowstone. This F. Jay Haynes photograph portrays the intense cold endured at Norris. Unfortunately, none of Bosse's sketches of the trip are known to have survived .

National Park Service

in the days when the park was mostly deserted in the winter.

The next morning dawned clear and cold (something less than 30 below zero), a perfect recipe for winter photography in Yellowstone. Photographer F. Jay Haynes, as he often penned his name, went out with some of the other members of the party and snowshoed around the nearby Norris Geyser Basin. In this case they did snowshoe in the contemporary sense of the term — the party apparently carried webbed snowshoes with them as they skied around the park. Haynes probably had discovered that generally webbed snowshoes do work better for photographing than do skis, since webbed 'shoes are usually used without poles and therefore leave one's hands free to manipulate photo gear. Haynes was thrilled by the lovely light and the profuse steam and frost, which he thought combined for form a scene that was "beautiful beyond description," and he shot some of the first of what would turn out to be a total of more than 40 photographs on this trip. While Haynes and the more able bodied members of the party were out exploring the winter wonderland around Norris Lieutenant Schwatka and the others hunkered close to the wood stove and rested in the Norris Hotel.

After spending just one full day at Norris, the entire party headed out on snowshoes of the Norwegian variety on the morning of the ninth. Their day's destination was the Firehole Hotel in the Lower Geyser Basin, a distance of 18 miles south on the way to Old Faithful, but according to accounts Schwatka was able to make it only four miles before he collapsed from exhaustion, his lungs gushing frightening fountains of blood. At that point, presumably in the vicinity of Gibbon Meadows, the leader of the expedition was forced to turn back to Norris in the escort of three others, at least two of whom apparently were also showing signs of being physically unable to perform. Haynes and the other eight members of the party continued on to the Lower Geyser Basin, where they were welcomed to the Firehole Hotel by the winterkeeper James Dean and his wife. The next morning, however, most of that segment of the party decided to return to Norris themselves. Perhaps they felt compelled to do so out of loyalty to Schwatka, perhaps they had seen enough of Yellowstone in winter, or perhaps they were simply overwhelmed by conditions. Whatever the cause, they did go back to the Norris Hotel as the whole expedition took on the appearance of a leaderless outfit losing its collective nerve in the face of adversity. All, that is, except for photographer Haynes and two others who decided to continue on to Old Faithful.

If judged provincially only in the context of his winter expedition to Yellowstone, it is easy to dismiss Frederick Schwatka as a self aggrandizing charlatan. With a closer look, however, it is evident that he had been the real deal in earlier chapters of his life. He had graduated from West Point in 1871, for example, and subsequently had been stationed on the Nebraska and Dakota frontier, and had managed to befriend some of the fierce Sioux in that area to the extent that they invited him to their sacred annual sun dance in 1875.

Then he had the courage to fight against the same tribe during the so called Great Sioux War of 1876, including the battles of Tongue River, the Rosebud, and Slim Buttes, and like his contemporary Lieutenant Gustavus Doane, it is conceivable that if things had been just a little different Schwatka could have had the misfortune to be with Custer at the wrong time and the wrong place at the Little Bighorn.

While stationed at remote outposts on the plains, he somehow managed to study for and to earn legal and medical degrees, which were awarded to him in consecutive years (1875 and 1876) from separate institutions. His first arctic expedition, an effort to find the Franklin Expedition of 1848 that had disappeared in while searching for the fabled Northwest Passage, spanned two years, and included a sledge journey of over 11 months duration and nearly 3,000 miles. This was regarded as a record distance for dogsled travel at the time. On that arctic trek it is notable, considering his later debacle in Yellowstone, that a major reason he was able to succeed was that he listened to the advice of natives, in this case the Inuit. Three years after the conclusion of his search for the remains of the Franklin Expedition, the U.S. Army dispatched Schwatka on a quasi military reconnaissance of the Yukon River through northwestern Canada and Alaska, and again he did well on the 1300 miles journey that was touted as another superlative of its day, this for being the longest raft journey ever made. In the months before his winter expedition into Yellowstone, he made another trip to Alaska, this one albeit an unsuccessful attempt to climb Mount St. Elias. Building on his achievements in the field, Schwatka also had found the time and energy to write extensively about his adventures on the western plains and in the arctic, and he had illustrated many of his writings with impressively rendered sketches done by his own hand.

And so it is quite a mystery why Schwatka refused to listen to local advice and failed so completely on his winter trip into Yellowstone. Perhaps some arrogance had grown from his previous successes, and perhaps prolonged exposure to severe arctic cold had damaged his lungs, a condition Yellowstone's high elevation and dry air would have aggravated. But a failure it was. After returning to the Norris Hotel after his collapse in Gibbon Meadows, Schwatka rested a few days, and then tried to snowshoe to Canyon. Presumably he regarded Canyon at a distance of 12 miles as something of a doable consolation after his failed attempt to negotiate the 30 mile trip to Old Faithful and the Upper Geyser Basin. But once again he managed only a short distance on the trail before he weakened and

had to return to Norris, although some of his party did continue on to Canyon where they spent one night with the Canyon winterkeepers before returning to Norris themselves.

On or about January 18, Schwatka and the segment of the party still with him skied back to Mammoth. This is striking, that after all their floundering on other legs of their trip that they were able to ski the entire 22 miles to Mammoth in one day. In full retreat psychologically as well as on the ground, their evacuation apparently gained momentum as it went along, like a runaway horse heading for the barn. In any event, Schwatka seems never to have recovered from his Yellowstone breakdown. He caught the last train out of Gardiner that winter, just before snowdrifts closed the spur line to the north, and in a few days was back at his home in Rock Island, Illinois. His subsequent endeavours were only moderately successful, and he was only 43 when he died just a little more than five years later. His death was due to an overdose of laudanum, which he was using to treat a stomach affliction, and was variously interpreted as accidental and as a suicide. The fact that Schwatka had been trained in medicine would seem to lend weight to the suicide side of that debate.

While Schwatka and the majority of the original expedition were recuperating at Norris and making their brief tour to Canyon, F. Jay Haynes and the two men who had stayed with him, whose names were Charles Stoddard and David Stratton and who apparently were some of the stronger members of the original group, had carried on to Old Faithful. They arrived there on the afternoon of January 10. Again they were greeted by a winterkeeper, in this case a man named James Roake, who was living at Old Faithful with his wife and family of four children, ranging in age from four to 14. The inescapable irony here, of course, is that winterkeepers were living at quite a few locations within the park and apparently were thriving, in some cases even with their wives and children, in the same environment that had overwhelmed the vaunted Schwatka and most of his crew.

Haynes and his group had been granted permission by the Yellowstone Park Association to stay in the Upper Geyser Basin Hotel near Old Faithful. Formal name aside, the hotel was popularly known as "The Shack," and winterkeeper Roake claimed that the building was so drafty that it was uninhabitable, so the wayfarers ended up staying in a tent pitched near Old Faithful Geyser. As its nickname would indicate, "The Shack" had a reputation for being poorly built, but one has to wonder whether there was some other reason why the winterkeeper did not want the travelers in the hotel, although in other regards Roake and his family were hospitable and he was the one who furnished the tent. But it would seem that any frame structure would have to be less drafty than any tent, and there is at least one winter photo of the building from the same time period in which it doesn't look that bad at all. Moreover, a tent pitched on geothermal ground anywhere is bound to be infiltrated by moisture emanating from the earth. It would further seem that, if nothing else, canvas from the tent or some other material could have been used to staunch the drafts in the hotel walls, or the tent could have been set up inside the building to combine with the frame walls against the frigid outside air. But stay in a tent the travelers did, and in all fairness photographer Haynes later related to his son that the accommodation was acceptably comfortable.

In keeping with the character of this record winter, a monstrous blizzard struck the Old Faithful area shortly after Haynes and his little party arrived, and they were pretty much confined to their tent for the next five days while the winds howled and heavy snow fell. The weather cleared on the night of January 15, and in the usual pattern following such a storm, the next morning dawned clear and intensely cold, a perfect morning for photography in the geyser basins. Of course Haynes was out early, unlimbering the bulky photography equipment he had steadfastly lugged so far. In another common pattern, luck came to the photographer who had put in his time, and he had the good fortune to see Old Faithful, Beehive, Giantess, Grand and Castle geysers erupt simultaneously. Haynes managed to photograph all but Grand before the eruptions ceased, quite a feat considering the cumbersome nature of the photography equipment of the time, and with the remainder of the day on the 16th and during a partial day on the 17th he shot a number of other memorable views of the Upper Basin.

Midday on the 17th Haynes and his party, which now included army scout Ed Wilson, skied back to the Firehole Hotel at the mouth of Nez Percé Creek on the first stage of their return journey north. Haynes had earlier recruited Wilson to assist his little party by telephoning the scout at his duty station at Mammoth.

Upper Geyser Basin Hotel, photographed by F. Jay Haynes in 1887, appears to be a substantial structure, but was nicknamed "The Shack" and pronounced uninhabitable by winterkeeper James Roake. Haynes and his party slept in tents during the sub-zero nights they spent at Old Faithful.

National Park Service

Yes, by 1887 most of the park was already linked by telephone, although service was intermittent because of wires downed by weather or falling trees. Telephone communication between developed locations — yet another reason to question just how much adventure or exploration was really involved in the ballyhooed Schwatka Expedition, even if it had been completed as planned. As an example of how winter travel in Yellowstone wasn't that big a deal if you knew how, scout Wilson apparently had skied solo from Mammoth to meet Haynes at Old Faithful. And the decision to return by traveling to Canyon via Norris marked a change in plans — originally the Schwatka Expedition had intended to travel from Old Faithful to Canyon via West Thumb and Lake. Perhaps Haynes and the others wanted to return to Norris to check on their erstwhile leader, but whatever the case Haynes did not see or photograph Yellowstone Lake on this trip.

Haynes and his three companions spent the night of the 17th with winterkeeper James Dean and his wife at the Firehole Hotel, and then rested there all the following day. The next morning they departed for Norris, which they reached after skiing the intervening 18 miles in one day without incident — they apparently were getting better at winter travel. They rested another full day at Norris, but they did not see Frederick Schwatka as the lieutenant and his contingent had already retreated north to Mammoth and ultimately out of the park. Haynes, Stoddard, Wilson and Stratton left Norris on the morning of January 20 to make the 12 mile journey east to Canyon, where they met with winterkeepers Al Thorne and Major

Lyman at the Canyon Hotel. Once again the wayfarers were beholden to winterkeepers for shelter from the harsh winter conditions.

During the next two days Haynes and the others skied around the area, especially along the North Rim of the Grand Canyon of the Yellowstone. Haynes and at least one other man also donned webbed snowshoes which they used to descend to Red Rock, and according to an account written much later by his son Jack, the photographer made a total of seven images in the area before getting weathered out on the afternoon of the 23rd. Members of the party noted that the spectacular colors of the canyon, so hypnotizing in summer, were buried under the snow. But they were most taken by the stunning ice formations created by spray from the Lower Falls, which up till and including Haynes's time often were referred to as the Great Falls of the Yellowstone River. Haynes described the falls as having "an ice bridge seventy-five to 100 feet thick" at its base, "while the north half of the falls is solid ice or huge icicles 200 feet long." In the later writing, his son added that the brink of the falls was "frozen over and hidden by an arch of ice about twelve feet thick." Haynes "secured a fine view" of the Great Falls from Red Rock, almost certainly the first photograph ever made of the Lower Falls in winter.

The next morning dawned at 21 below zero at Canyon, an indication that the cloudiness that had abbreviated Haynes' shooting the day before had been transitory and that as a consequence temperatures had dropped sharply under clear skies. Under those clear skies Haynes and his three companions left Canyon bound for Yancey's Hotel near Tower Junction. The distance they had to travel was only about 20 miles, but the route was over the Washburn Mountain Range and at its highest point, their trail would be more than 10,000 feet in elevation. They had no way of knowing it when they left Canyon, but their trip would become one of the great epic journeys in Yellowstone history. There is no question that the four adventurers had been getting better at winter travel — remember, they had skied the 12 miles from Norris to Canyon in about a half day — but now it seems that their new comfort level had inspired an excessive confidence. They set off on their crossing of the Washburn Range as though it was going to be a half day lark, with food for only one lunch and almost no survival gear.

Charles Stoddard and David Stratton, the two men who had been in the original Schwatka party and who had continued with Haynes since the photographer had set off on his own after Schwatka's collapse on January 9, were local men from Livingston, Montana. They should have known something about regional weather, especially about how quickly conditions in the mountains can change from comparatively mild to lethally threatening in the winter. Haynes himself had been coming to Yellowstone since 1881, and while his experiences here had been in summer only, it seems that he should have absorbed something from someone about the potential dangers of winter at such high elevations. And most of all, Ed Wilson the scout should have seen to it that the little party was better prepared for their January crossing of the Washburns.

Winterkeepers, with their dog, shoveling snow from the roof of the first Canyon Hotel, January 1887 (right). Photographer Haynes, Stoddard, Stratton and Wilson sheltered in this hotel during their time at Canyon. The opposite end of the building in summer (below) gives perspective to how much snow the winterkeepers had piled up under the eaves of the hotel.

HOTEL AT THE GRAND CANYON.

National Park Service

Although Wilson apparently had just arrived in Yellowstone (in 1885), he was described as having been a trapper and generally a rugged outdoorsman in his earlier life. Indeed, he was so highly regarded by the park's official establishment that he had been hired as a "mountaineer assistant" upon his arrival here, and he was subsequently promoted the next year as just the second scout in the park's history. On top of all these considerations, by now all four of the men had been in the park for 19 days, and had experienced firsthand a lot of what Yellowstone's winter can be in terms of wind, snow and arctic temperatures. Perhaps Wilson or the others did offer cautionary advice to Haynes, and Haynes threw their caution to the wind for fear of emulating Schwatka's defeatist example, or out of an innate sense of personal determination. But there really was no excuse for setting out as half cocked as the party did on such a perilous crossing. They all should have known better.

The party's first objective that morning was the summit of Mount Washburn, which they apparently accomplished. But a short time after they began their descent from the peak the clear skies clouded over and yet another blizzard commenced, with the usual mix of frigid temperatures, falling snow, and strong winds which blew and drifted the powdery snow that would have been especially light and fluffy at that elevation. In a short time all landmarks were obscured and all the skiers were totally disoriented. As often occurs in such situations, it evidently didn't occur to the party to turn around and retrace their back trail to Canyon until the tracks had been buried under the falling and drifting snow, or perhaps the storm may have come on so violently that it would have been impossible to go back up and over the top of the 10,243 foot mountain. In spite of the splendid panoramic views available from the top of Mount Washburn, Haynes significantly shot no photographs from the summit, so maybe the explorers could see that a change in weather was in the offing and they felt the need to hustle down to lower elevations.

As it was the little party spent the remainder of the daylight period lurching about somewhere between the top of Mount Washburn and Rowland Pass, the notch on the east or opposing side of the mountain from the better known Dunraven Pass. Darkness arrived and the oversights they had made in preparing for their trek between Canyon and Tower came back to haunt them. They had no tent, no blankets and only a couple of biscuits apiece and a little chocolate for food. Perhaps the grossest oversight of all, given the way things unfolded, is that they apparently had

National Park Service

Yellowstone's pioneering photographer F. Jay Haynes on his winter trip through the park in January of 1887. The anorak Haynes wore likely came from Lt. Frederick Schwatka, who had spent time with the Inuit in the Arctic.

no compass. They did manage to find a modicum of shelter in a clump of krummholz trees that at least one account of the ordeal describes as growing in an enclosed circle. These would undoubtedly have been subalpine firs, and especially near the timberline the species sometimes does grow in a circular pattern, with what appear to be offspring trees growing in a ring under the drip line of a parent tree. In some cases the parent tree dies and leaves a vacancy in the middle of the copse of smaller trees, and it was in such a boreal arrangement that the wayfarers took refuge. For additional protection from the wind they dug a pit in the snow with their snowshoes, and managed to kindle a fire in the bottom of the pit.

According to some accounts, the storm continued unabated the next day; other accounts say the storm had eased but that a dense fog enveloped the mountains. Either way, the skiers could not determine where they were and spent the day trudging an estimated 20 miles that gained them nothing but another night in another snowbank. Their second night out was worse than the first, with added fatigue and further deprivation of sustenance coupled with the fact that this nightfall found them on an open slope with no trees for shelter or firewood. The lost travelers later reported that they suffered hallucinations while hopping around in the darkness to keep warm, and one of the party "nearly succumbed." Throughout their time in the Washburns they frequently heard the ominous roar of avalanches sweeping down the slopes, the terror of which was heightened by the fact that they just couldn't see. One of their nights out was reported to be 52 degrees below zero. This was probably their second night, when the weather cleared and the extreme cold that accompanied the clearing skies nearly did them in. But of course the clear weather is also what saved them the next day, because "all knew the country well in a clear atmosphere," and when they could see what they were doing they were able to navigate down Antelope Creek to Tower with no further complications other than their own exhaustion. They arrived at Yancey's Hotel in the late afternoon of January 25, where "Uncle" John Yancey fed and sheltered the wayfarers for two nights and one full day, after which they made an uneventful trip back to Mammoth Hot Springs on the 27th. Haynes shot a picture of the group in front of Yancey's just before they departed for Mammoth.

David Stratton and Charles Stoddard apparently never had any more noteworthy experiences in Yellowstone. Ed Wilson quickly became an accomplished scout, drawing on his experiences with the Haynes expedition to become an expert at winter patrol, to the point where his specialty became the ability to navigate around the wintry park through storminess and the dark of night as a cover for sneaking up on poachers. As valued as he was for what he could do, Wilson unfortunately seems to have gone the way of many law enforcement types in that he suspected everyone of wrongdoing, even his fellow park employees, and consequently wound up socially isolated. Then in 1891 he fell in love with a beautiful woman who did not reciprocate his interest. By July 27 of that year "he was suffering from aberration of mind," as it was put on a reward poster in search of Wilson after he went missing, and he committed suicide by taking an overdose of morphine. Even though he died on a hill overlooking park headquarters at Mammoth, his body was not discovered for nearly a year.

The F. Jay Haynes party departing from Yancey's Hotel on January 27, 1887, after spending two nights and one full day at the establishment recuperating from their frigid ordeal in the Washburn Range on their trip from Canyon.

F. Jay Haynes, of course, continued a long and eminently successful career as Yellowstone's official photographer, as well as a prominent park concessionaire until his death in 1921; his son Jack continued the family tradition in Yellowstone until his own death in 1962. The elder Haynes shot over 40 images on his 1887 winter trip, and he would take additional winter tours and make additional winter photos in subsequent years. To his credit, his comrades from the 1887 trip spoke "in glowing terms of the professor [as Haynes was often called], who is as cool and self-preserved in the hour of peril as when in his studio." Another chronicler of the junket wrote that "[Haynes] was perfectly self-possessed during the whole journey, never complained, was always ready to take his place and perform his share of the duties of the hour." Of the trip, Haynes himself would write "I have just completed the only series of 'Mid-Winter Views of Wonderland' ever made...the interesting and beautiful results of several weeks' perilous work, during January last, in that wonderful region, making the entire circuit of the Park (nearly two hundred miles) on snowshoes."

"I prefer to make most of my trips alone."
— Billy Hofer

VII

Cross Country Skis Arrive In Yellowstone

"From here to there on boards"

Thermal mist frozen on tree boughs at Norris Geyser Basin

Only about three and a half weeks after Frederick Schwatka returned from his ineffectual outing into Yellowstone, a man named Thomas Elwood Hofer embarked on a trip of his own into the park. Hofer, who was commonly know as "Uncle Billy," was a correspondent on assignment for Forest and Stream Magazine, and he planned a course around the park quite similar to the one that Schwatka had planned but had not accomplished. The similarities between the two men and their respective trips into Yellowstone ended about there, however. Like many of his contemporaries as well as most Yellowstone locals since that time, Hofer was filled with disdain for Schwatka:

"There is much humbug about the whole thing [Schwatka's expedition]. As well talk of "exploring" Central Park, New York, as the National Park. The National Park is well known country; everything worth seeing is mapped out and described in reports and geological surveys, guide books and newspaper letters. The extent of the Schwatka "explorations" consisted in following a first-class wagon road, 30 ft. wide, cut through the forest, and planted with telephone poles every 200 feet."

Elsewhere in his writings Hofer related another anecdote about Schwatka and his showmanship, this one having to do with a bottle that Hofer noticed suspended 12 feet above the level on the snow on a tree near the camp Schwatka had established near Indian Creek on one of his first nights of his expedition into the park. Hofer salvaged the bottle because he wanted to use it to carry liquid refreshment on his own trip, but upon closer inspection he found that Schwatka had written a note on the label of the vessel. In the note Schwatka claimed that the snow was as deep as the spot on the tree where the bottle had been placed, and that the temperature at the time was 51 degrees below zero. Hofer apparently did some subsequent research, and discovered that on the date the bottle had been left by Lieutenant Schwatka (January 7), the snow had been about three feet deep at the site, and the recorded temperatures at Mammoth Hot Springs and at the Lower Geyser Basin had been -26 and -31 degrees, respectively. Hofer added that *"I suppose that the snow must have been very deep when the bottle was 'placed on the level of the snow,' and the weather very much colder here than anywhere else in the Park. As there was nothing in the bottle but air I concluded that the whole thing was a misstatement and that the high winds had blown and lodged the bottle in the tree, even with a telephone insulator on the other side of the tree. Strange things happen in the Park."*

As the above quotes would indicate, Billy Hofer was a no-nonsense sort of man who devoted a long career to Yellowstone. He first arrived in 1877, and for the next 50 years he worked as a guide, a correspondent, an advanced amateur photographer, and sometimes as a scout for the government. He claimed to have made his first winter trip into the park proper as early as 1880. Over his years in Yellowstone, Hofer also operated several concessions in the park, but unfortunately for him none of these was very successful, and he wound up living out his last years not only in poverty but also removed to the state of Washington from his beloved Yellowstone. The purpose of the winter trip he commenced in mid February of 1887 was to survey wintering wildlife, especially bison; this was the first ever such survey in Yellowstone's history. He chose only one companion to accompany him on the circuit, a man named Jack Tansey. Having even one companion was something of an exception for the capable Hofer, who had a taste for independent travel. Hofer had a bit of a judgmental edge about him that was born from confidence in his own abilities, but it's hard not to like him at the points where his love for Yellowstone shines through. Soon after departing from Mammoth, for example, Hofer and Tansey sighted some wintering elk in Gardner's Hole. So exuberant was Hofer at the sight that he "could not resist the temptation to shout, and I gave one whoopee! I think every elk heard it and started for higher ground: not knowing what was wrong, they collected on some high points, where they remained so long as in sight." Emerging from the steep and closed in climb from Mammoth onto the broad panorama of Gardner's Hole is always exhilarating, elk or no elk. This is especially true in winter when unmarred snowscapes spread out in the foreground and lead the eye to the brilliant whiteness of the Gallatin Range in the distance, and the winter traveler facing into an icy wind realizes that this is the beginning of the Yellowstone plateau's vast sweep of snow. Hofer's exuberance is understandable, and he can be forgiven for whatever disturbance he might have caused the elk.

Hofer and Tansey's route basically followed Yellowstone's Grand Loop Road. That had been Schwatka's original plan, too, but with Hofer and Tansey the southern end of the loop expanded westward off the roadway to take in the DeLacy Creek drainage and the eastern edge of Shoshone Lake. They made detailed observations about the wildlife they saw along the way, not just about the large herbivores that had been assigned as the principal objective of their trip, but about birds and smaller animals as well. Now, well over a century later, we find their observations interesting because of the differences between what they saw and what we see today. For instance, they saw

very little in the way of large herbivores in the geyser basins on the west side, where we in more recent times have seen large numbers of such animals. And in many different locations they found a great deal of wolverine and lynx sign, two animals that are extremely rare in Yellowstone nowadays.

They also saw several elk and signs of a lot more in Hayden Valley, a harshly wintry part of the park where no elk winter today. Notably, they also reported a group of ten elk living along the rim of the Grand Canyon, but it seems that those elk had made a mistake in selecting that location for winter habitation, as at least two of them had ventured so far out beyond the rim of good footing that they had fallen to their deaths into the canyon shortly before Hofer and Tansey arrived in the area. To be sure, those two elk had fallen while in panicked flight from the local hotel winterkeepers, who thought the elk could not survive in the canyon and with good intentions were trying to drive the animals to what the men thought was better habitat. An interesting parallel to this 1887 observation of elk in the Canyon area occurred in a much more recent winter, that of 2001-2002. During that winter several radio collared cow elk who theretofore had spent nonmigratory lives in the Firehole River drainage just north of Old Faithful were displaced by growing pressure from wolves and suddenly left their home range to end up along the rims of the Grand Canyon of the Yellowstone, about 40 miles away. Claire Gower, a PhD student at the time and one of the biologists whose task it was to keep track of the collared elk, interpreted the movement as predator avoidance, but the elk that fled to Canyon in 2002 didn't fare much better than the ones who tried to winter there 115 years earlier---within a fairly short time they were all dead from one cause or another, although none of the twenty-first century elk is known to have fallen to its death. It is interesting to speculate that in both cases the elk who tried to winter at Canyon did so in off-balance reaction to rather abrupt changes in Yellowstone---European settlement and non-sustainable levels of hunting pressure in the surrounding area in the case of the earlier group and the reintroduction of wolves (in 1995) to Yellowstone National Park in the case of the second group. While this last thought is pure speculation, it is unquestionably true that Canyon is not a good place for elk to winter, and for the overwhelming majority of recorded years, no elk have stayed there beyond late autumn.

Among his other observations, Hofer used his ski pole to take frequent soundings of snow depths along

An 1894 F. Jay Haynes photograph (above) shows Billy Hofer shouldering his skis and wading Alum Creek, a geothermal stream in Hayden Valley that never freezes. The photograph inspired famed western artist Frederic Remington to sketch Hofer in a similar scene (right). Hofer had been hired to guide Haynes and others on the 1894 trip, the purpose of which was to survey wintering wildlife in the park.

his route. In keeping with the nature of that record winter, and consistent with the view that Yellowstone's winters were snowier in those days, he recorded some truly impressive figures. He found four and half to five feet on the ground near the junction of Indian Creek and the Gardiner River, for example, which is not a particularly snowy part of the park. In the vicinity of Norris, he claimed the snow was seven feet deep on the level, and that a drift by the Norris Hotel was as high as the second story. At the Firehole Hotel in the Lower Geyser Basin winterkeeper James Dean, who had sheltered Haynes and his party two different times the previous month, related to him that the season's snowfall to date (February 18) had totaled 12'9." Bear in mind that the latter figure is for snowfall, and that total would have settled down to a much lower figure in terms of snowpack. But again, neither Norris Junction nor the Lower Geyser Basin is considered especially snowy in a relative sense, and for those two locations Hofer's totals would be very high end by today's standards. And then at Old Faithful Hofer and Tansey found winterkeeper James Roake and his family living in a cabin that was almost completely

buried except for its stovepipe, which itself barely extended above the snow. Roake also had a total for the season's snowfall, which he told Hofer amounted to 15'10" in the Upper Geyser Basin. This would be a logical amount in a relative sense to the figure given to Hofer by Dean for the Lower Basin, which as its name suggests is a bit lower in elevation than the Upper Basin, so it seems likely that the two winterkeepers were making fairly accurate observations. Roake added that the house he and his family lived in had indeed been totally buried before the fluffy new snow had consolidated to the seven feet of snowpack that Hofer found when he arrived at Old Faithful. Hofer and Tansey stayed in a tent at Old Faithful, almost certainly the same one where Haynes and his party had lodged earlier in the winter. Hofer added a tidbit that the tent had been set up at Old Faithful "ever since the old Y.P.I. started." Taken literally, that would mean since the inception of the Yellowstone Park Improvement Company in 1883. Hofer did not explain how the tent had managed to hold up under the snowloads of that and previous winters, but like Haynes he did mention that he and Tansey were able to make themselves comfortable in the canvas abode.

When they left Old Faithful bound for Shoshone Lake Hofer and Tansey had to cross the Continental Divide somewhere east of Lone Star Geyser, and then had to cross the Divide again when they left Shoshone Lake for the West Thumb of Yellowstone Lake. Not only were the trekkers at high elevation, that segment of their route also took them closer to the south and west sides of the park, so they were in some of the snowier parts of the park. Hofer could no longer take accurate depth soundings, as his ski pole was only seven feet long and snow depths on that part of their trek easily exceeded that. En route from Shoshone Lake to Yellowstone Lake, the men encountered a heavy, swirling snowfall, to the point where Hofer had to rely on his compass to navigate through the thickly timbered country. It may be remembered that the Haynes party suffered greatly for want of a compass on their crossing of the Washburn Range a few weeks earlier---Hofer was much more experienced and better prepared. It was slow going for the two skiers on

this part of the route, with Hofer calculating their average rate of progress at one and a quarter miles per hour. While Hofer was charitable in his references to his companion Jack Tansey, by reading between the lines it does seem that the less experienced man slowed Hofer to some extent. In one of his earlier writings, Hofer had noted that "I prefer to make most of my trips alone," and Hofer must have reflected on that philosophy during the long, slow trudges.

Arriving at Yellowstone Lake around midday on February 24, the travelers used hot spring water from West Thumb Geyser Basin to reconstitute some of the soup stock provided to them during their layover at Old Faithful by James Roake and his family. (Again, where would these early travelers in wintry Yellowstone have been without the help of winterkeepers?) After eating their lunch, the men struck off across the ice of Yellowstone Lake in a driving storm, which blew at them from the southwest the way a similar storm had blown at Lieutenant Gustavus Doane and his men in the same part of the lake a little over a decade before, in the early winter of 1876. The storm caused visibility problems for Hofer and Tansey, so maybe Uncle Billy had to use his compass again to stay on course. Their more immediate concerns, however, were ski conditions. Almost anyone who has ever skied across Yellowstone Lake has had the sobering experience of planting a ski pole in what was expected to be dry snow, only to have the pole come up dripping with water hidden under the snow but lurking on top of the ice. Ice on the lake heaves and cracks into huge plates in a manner somewhat reminiscent, on an infinitesimally smaller scale, of the way ice in the great Yellowstone glacier strained against itself when

© Jeff Henry

Billy Hofer's fertile imagination saw all manner of fanciful creatures formed in the frost-laden ghost trees of Yellowstone's thermal basins. He wrote about frost-formed sculptures of "...hogs, rabbits, mules, elephants, leopards, tigers, cats, animals of all kinds and shapes, creatures that outside the park nothing but a disordered mind could conjure up." Hofer also saw images of people in the ghost trees. Some were women speaking to groups of children, or of two women quarreling with each other. For example, the top of the ghost tree pictured here has a profile that might be that of a woman sternly pointing, perhaps while lecturing her children, or to make a point in an argument. Of course, the forms in the frost are just frost, and can be made to fit almost anything that preexists in the onlooker's mind.

© Jeff Henry

A strong blizzard was blowing in the West Thumb of Yellowstone Lake when Billy Hofer and his companion skied across the ice there in late February of 1887. Apparently Hofer was unaware of Carrington Island, for when he first saw the little trees on the little island through the blowing snow he thought he was seeing the forms of wild animals. This was how Carrignton Island looked one morning in March of 1999. Mount Sheridan looms out of the frozen fog in the distance.

it was centered on the same basin during Pinedale glaciation times. In the latter day phenomenon water wells up through the cracks in the ice, which can be several feet deep in cold winters, and then seeps laterally between the ice plates and the overlying snow. Usually more scary than truly dangerous, the water is always inconvenient, since it flash freezes to skis and poles as soon as it is exposed to free flowing air and inevitably necessitates a stop to scrape things clean. Hofer may have been the first to speculate that it is the weight of the snow on top of the ice that forces liquid water upward through the cracks between ice plates. He may have been the first, but many other skiers on the lake in the years since Hofer's time have come up with the same interpretation.

That night they made it only as far as the north shore of West Thumb, where they camped, and then continued the next day by returning to the ice and skiing parallel to the north shore of the channel connecting West Thumb to the main body of the lake. Another gale was blowing, but in this case they were close enough to shore for easy navigation, and the wind was at their backs and actually helped them along because "at every step we could gain a little extra distance by the aid of the wind." At the Sand Point-Rock Point area they found that the wind had abated somewhat and they once again struck off across a large expanse of ice toward the lake outlet at Fishing Bridge, which they reached with enough daylight left to ski two miles farther down the river below the lake.

From that camp the next morning they skied across Hayden Valley to Canyon, where they put up with the same winterkeepers (Major Lyman and Al Thorne) who had hosted F. Jay Haynes and his party earlier in the winter. In both Hayden Valley and at Canyon the surveyors saw the elk that seem so out of place when viewed from today's perspective, noting that one bull that was close enough for them to see in detail was "quite poor." After spending four days at Canyon, Hofer and Tansey skied over the Washburn Range toward Yancey's Hotel at Tower Junction on March 3. In contrast with the Haynes group, Hofer saw to it that he and Tansey took sufficient food and gear and they made the mountain crossing without incident, camping out for one "very comfortable night" on the way. They were warmly received by Uncle John, who had heard through the Yellowstone grapevine that they were coming, but they stayed at his hotel only one night, after which they made the uneventful 19 mile ski back to Mammoth to complete their trip. On the way back to Mammoth, Hofer and Tansey noticed the tracks of horse drawn sleigh traffic that had been traveling on the road, at least until recently.

Hofer and Tansey did not haul the bulky photographic equipment that the Haynes party did, and they did not make the extra effort required to do the photographic work, but they did make the effort required to record detailed notes about the wildlife they saw along the way, and they skied a considerably longer route than had the earlier party. In all, Hofer displayed much greater skill and preparedness than had either the Schwatka party or its Haynes offshoot, and this is especially true when considering that Jack Tansey was not experienced in the wintry environment of the park and most importantly was a novice skier, so in addition to planning ahead, navigating and doing everything else necessary to manage such a trip Hofer had to keep an eye on his green companion.

Hofer had gained his experience on skis before he came to Yellowstone by spending 10 years carrying mail between mining camps in Colorado. By all accounts, that is how skis arrived in America---with Scandinavian transplants using the accoutrements to shuttle mail and other critical commodities between snowbound mining communities, possibly beginning with John "Snowshoe" Thompson in California's Mother Lode country in 1856. Hofer was one of the first to arrive in the Yellowstone area with ski experience, but he wasn't the first. According to famed Yellowstone historian Aubrey Haines in his landmark book The Yellowstone Story, the earliest recorded use of Norwegian snowshoes in the area was by A.

Bart Henderson in December of 1872 when he skied on "fifteen foot snowshoes" from his ranch near Gardiner to Bozeman for a Christmas party. Henderson himself had been a prospector in the Yellowstone area since 1866, so if he was using skis by 1872 it is likely that others in the prospecting and mining fraternity were skiing as well. This would have been especially likely among the miners working in the richly mineralized Cooke City/Clark's Fork area outside the park's northeast corner. For the most part, miners operating there originated in southwestern Montana and used towns like Bozeman and Helena as bases of supply. Traveling in the direction of those towns took the miners across the northern tier of Yellowstone and skis would have been useful accessories on that route in the winter. Remember, A. Bart Henderson used skis to go to Bozeman, and he began his trip from the vicinity of Gardiner, about 3,500 feet lower in elevation and much less snowy than the mountains around the Cooke City mines. Skis also would have been helpful for travel within the New World mining district, as the area came to be called, where snow cover lasts for more than half the year.

Incidentally, those New World miners were notorious poachers in the park, and their infringements were largely responsible for the appearance of another legendary figure on the Yellowstone stage. Harry Yount was hired with the title of gamekeeper and stationed in a cabin at the junction of Soda Butte Creek and Lamar River for the winter of 1880-1881 "so as to protect the game, especially elk and bison, in their sheltered chosen winter haunts, from the Clark's Fork and other miners," as Yount himself put it. "Rocky Mountain Harry" was a fascinating character from a

"Rocky Mountain Harry," or Harry Yount, hired as gamekeeper in Yellowstone in 1880. Yount spent the winter of 1880-1881 in a cabin near the junction of Soda Butte Creek and Lamar River, looking after wintering wildlife in that area.

family with a long history of pioneering in America, with elements of his family having settled the raw frontiers of New York, Pennsylvania, North Carolina, Missouri and California. Yount himself carried on the family tradition and was a "typical leatherstocking frontiersman," who was further described as "rough, tough and intelligent." He first came to Wyoming right after the Civil War, in which he had served bravely, suffered a leg wound, and spent time as a prisoner of war. Although he stayed in Wyoming for most of the last six decades of his life, less than two years of that time was actually spent in Yellowstone National Park. In spite of the short duration of his service here, his impacts on the park and the future National Park Service were large. Yount is widely regarded as a prototype for later park rangers, who didn't appear on the scene until after the creation of the National Park Service in 1915. Nowadays there is even a prestigious park ranger award that is named in his honor. Younts Peak, a massive mountain that forms the ultimate head of the Yellowstone River about 20 miles south of the southeast corner of Yellowstone National Park, is also named for him.

Yount's winter in Lamar Valley distinguishes him as being one of the first people that we know for sure spent a winter in the park. He lived alone for most of that winter, save for occasional visits by Adam "Horn" Miller and George Rowland, two acquaintances of Yount's from the Cooke City area. Much of Yount's own career was spent in occupations related to mining, and that is probably the reason that he apparently knew how to ski. Of particular interest to this book is a notation Yount made in the 1881 Yellowstone Superintendent's report. In recounting what he knew of the park's bison from his experiences during the winter of 1880-1881, Yount wrote "I found…that a small band of bison wintered on Alum Creek [in Hayden Valley] and another on the South Fork [Firehole River] of the Madison River…." As tempting as it is to think that this entry meant that the gamekeeper had made a mid winter trip around the park, Yount's writing elsewhere in his report strongly implies that he learned these tidbits about the bison from a late winter/early spring trip, after travel and weather conditions had eased a bit. He does clearly state, however, that he used snowshoes for at least part of his bison-counting trip or trips to Hayden Valley and the Firehole River. Given the nomenclature of his time, Yount almost certainly meant the Norwegian snowshoe, or what we would call the cross country ski, rather than the webbed or Canadian snowshoe.

So it appears that the most likely route that skis followed to the Yellowstone area was with people like A. Bart Henderson, Uncle Billy Hofer and Rocky Mountain Harry Yount who had been involved in the mining business elsewhere in the West. Skis proved as practical here as they had in other mineralized areas, most of which tended to be high in the mountains and therefore snowy, and they caught on just as quickly here as they had in other places. Mail carriers, winterkeepers and poachers were some of the people who found skis pretty much indispensable for winter in Yellowstone. Two of the people who have figured prominently in recent pages of this book, Uncle Billy Hofer and the scout Ed Wilson, also figured prominently in introducing the art of cross country skiing to the recently arrived United States Army. The ski patrols the army sent into Yellowstone over the next 30 years are such a romantic episode in the park's history that they deserve their own chapter.

As some before and many more since his time, Billy Hofer was taken by the endless contrasts between fire and ice in wintry Yellowstone. In Norris Geyser Basin he observed "boiling water and solid ice within less than a foot of each other."

© Jeff Henry

One of the chief concerns of the cavalry's winter ski patrols was the welfare of Yellowstone's bison herd. For a time in the late 19th and early 20th centuries the park's remnant herd faced the very real threat of outright elimination by poaching, most of which occurred during the winter when snow left the animals less mobile and easier for poachers to find.

© Jeff Henry

VIII

United States Army in Yellowstone

"Dismounted Cavalry on Cross Country Skis"

Jerry Brekke

Fort Yellowstone soldier's cap

Yellowstone National Park was created on March 1, 1872, and spent the first 14 1/2 years of its existence under civilian administration. Funding for the new park, however, was always spotty, and in the summer of 1886 a congressional debate over the future evolution of the reserve — a strong contingent wanted to do away with the park altogether — led to a slashing of funds to pay the salaries of the small force of civilian administrators and overseers on hand. Most of those people quit abruptly and left Yellowstone when they learned of the budget shortfall that was to deny them compensation, and for much of the summer the park was left largely unprotected. The park no longer was blessed by the isolation that it had enjoyed just a few years earlier, and predictable violations took place in the absence of oversight. Vandalistic tourists hammered away at geothermal features, using metal tools to engrave their names and to pry specimens from the formations, while various local residents who harbored resentments of one sort or another against the new park took advantage of the situation to cut timber and to poach game inside the reserve. The unfettered opportunity to poach probably was enjoyed with special relish, since hunting in the park had been outlawed just three years earlier and its prohibition was the cause of much of the resentment felt toward the reserve in surrounding communities. Finally, in a fortunate turn of fate late in the summer of 1886, the United States Cavalry was called in to pick up the slack and save the national park.

Defaced thermal features and wildlife poaching aside, the arriving cavalry's most immediate concern was how to do deal with wildfires. Tourists leaving unattended campfires were responsible for some of the fires burning out of control in the park when the army showed up. And in acts of particular malice, some fires had been set intentionally by especially disgruntled locals, who were described to the commander of the arriving troops by outgoing civilian superintendent David Wear as "unscrupulous" and as a certain "class of frontiersmen, hunters, trappers, and squaw men." The most obvious of the deliberate fires had been set on the north side of Bunsen Peak, the side of the mountain facing Mammoth, so the blaze was in plain view of the soldiers and must have had a commanding presence over them as they set up their camp at park headquarters near the hot springs. It goes without saying that the summer 1886 must have been dry, or else the park wouldn't have been burning regardless of the sources of ignition. The following winter, of course, was the historically heavy winter of 1886-1887, and the pattern of a snowy winter frequently following on the heels of a dry summer has been discernible throughout Yellowstone's history, up to and including the present time.

The army unit assigned to guard Yellowstone was Company M of the First Cavalry Regiment, and the commander who met Superintendent Wear upon arriving at Mammoth was Captain Moses Harris. Harris must have been a physically brave man, having enlisted in the Union army as a teenager when the Civil War broke out in 1861. He had fought with distinction in that great war, achieving officer rank by the end of the conflict and also winning the Congressional Medal of Honor. He also had been wounded in the war and as a consequence spent the rest of his life with a disfigured face. In addition to personal bravery, Harris was elsewhere described as creative, determined and resourceful, but something in his personal makeup left him almost completely unlikable, to the point where for much of his time at Mammoth he didn't dare venture outside his quarters after dark. As one man who knew him wrote from a long retrospective, Harris had both a mean nature and a mean look, and that "he had no friends, but all were his enemies." Captain Harris had never been to Yellowstone before he arrived officially, at the head of his First Cavalry detail.

The company he commanded and the regiment of which it was a part already had a long history in the United States Army, tracing its antecedents back as far as 1833. The unit had fought in the Mexican War, various Indian wars during the antebellum period, and then in the Civil War itself. After the Civil War the regiment returned to the West where it had engaged in several more Indian actions; the regiment had been especially murderous of Modoc Indians during the Modoc War of 1872-1873, and of Apaches in Arizona between the late 1860s and the mid 1880s. In late 1885 the unit had been transferred from the desert southwest to Fort Custer in Montana Territory, at the junction of the Bighorn and Yellowstone rivers. They had been at their new post in Montana for only about a year when they received orders to march to Yellowstone and assume protection of the new park. In a loose parallel with John Colter, the post the soldiers left behind when they marched off to Yellowstone was situated almost exactly in the same strategic place where Manuel Lisa's fur trading post had been located when the legendary mountain man set out from there on his trek through Yellowstone 79 years earlier.

This seemingly curious course of affairs, where the military wound up protecting the national park, came about for several reasons. The first was that a few years earlier congressional friends of Yellowstone had anticipated the budgetary strategy against the park that materialized in 1886, and they had laid the legislative groundwork for allowing the army to assume control of the reservation in lieu of a civilian administration which had been drawn down financially. The second was that influential members of the military itself, officers like Generals Phil Sheridan and William T. Sherman, had visited Yellowstone previously and had enjoyed positive experiences there. As a corollary to the generals' favorable disposition toward the park, some of the social elite of the time had begun to enjoy sport hunting as an expression of social standing. This social subset, which included many high ranking officers of the army itself, envisioned a Yellowstone that functioned as a reservoir of game animals that could be hunted by themselves and their cohorts when the excess populations migrated out of the park. For these and other reasons the military establishment was willing to cooperate and send Captain Harris and the 50 men of M Company to Yellowstone, where they arrived in the evening of August 17, 1886. Initially the soldiers were under the impression that their stay in Yellowstone would be rather brief, but the army presence was destined to continue in the park for 32 years.

Upon arrival in Yellowstone, Captain Harris dispatched some number of his troop, perhaps 12 to 18 men, to man six different duty stations around the park; the interior duty stations were located at or near the principal points of interest in the reserve. Much of the effort of the remaining members of his outfit was devoted to fighting wildfires, which Harris viewed as his top priority. At first the troop merely set up a tent camp for themselves, but word came to Captain Harris in September that his unit was to stay in Yellowstone through the following winter, and that they were to "provide such temporary shelter for the command as may be necessary for the comfort of the troops and the protection of public property." In spite of the word "temporary," Harris must have realized that to survive the Rocky Mountain winter, even at Mammoth's relatively low elevation, he would have to construct some fairly substantial shelter for his men, their equipment, and their horses. He also must have realized that with autumn already upon them, time for completing the construction of this new highest priority was short. Considering how his small company was scattered about the park, fighting fires and attending to other new duties in a strange environment, an old military maxim might have occurred to Captain Harris, that "To divide one's forces in time of peril is to invite piecemeal destruction." But by November first all the soldiers stationed at the outlying posts, with the exception of one contingent left at Soda Butte to look after the game-rich Lamar Valley, had been recalled to Mammoth and somehow the reassembled Company

M did succeed in finishing five buildings by the end of December. The new buildings included a barracks for the men, a storehouse, a guardhouse, a stable for their horses, and a quartermaster facility. It must have been cold work, wielding hammers and saws in the Yellowstone autumn and early winter, but at the end of it the soldiers at least had set themselves up with a base in their new home.

Their home in Yellowstone must have been new indeed. Since the Civil War the First Cavalry Regiment had been stationed primarily on the West Coast and in the desert southwest. Yellowstone was not an exceptionally remote duty station by the standards existing in 1886, but it certainly was different in other important ways than say, The Presidio in San Francisco or Fort McDowell in Arizona Territory, two examples of posts where the unit had been stationed in the years leading up to their park assignment. The biggest difference for the men soon after their arrival would have been the wintry nature of the park. Undoubtedly, some of the soldiers had come from wintry parts of the country, and some of the duty stations where the First Cavalry had been stationed previously experience some degree of winter, but it is almost certain that none of the men had lived or worked in an environment so dominated by deep snow. In Yellowstone the lasting snows came in late October or early November. In most of the park the snow didn't melt significantly until April or even May — it just got deeper and deeper on the ground as the winter went along. The cavalry's horses were no good in such a place, and you couldn't walk through such snow, either — it was soft and fluffy and higher than your head. Of course the answer was snowshoes, both the webbed and the Norwegian varieties. Fortunately for the troopers of Company M, there were people on the Yellowstone scene who had experience with both types of 'shoes and could instruct the soldiers on their use.

One such person was Collins Jack Baronett, better known as "Yellowstone Jack." Baronett had been born in Scotland in 1829, and first arrived in the Yellowstone area in 1864. In his years before coming to Yellowstone he had been a sailor on the high seas, had fought for the South in the American Civil War, and for a short time had been employed as a mercenary in Mexico. In the greater Yellowstone area he had been a prospector for gold and a scout for the army, even scouting for General Custer at times. He also had fought against the Sioux along the Bozeman Trail, and generally he was considered a first rate frontiersman. Among his accomplishments in the immediate park area was the bridge he constructed across the Yellowstone River. Built during the winter of 1870-1871, Baronett's bridge was the first to be constructed across the river, not just within the boundaries of the future park but anywhere along its course. The toll bridge was on the Yellowstone near its junction with Lamar River, and its purpose was to serve traffic going back and forth between the Cooke City mines and southwestern Montana towns like Bozeman, which the miners used as supply centers. As pointed out previously, it was likely miners who first introduced the concept of skiing in the Yellowstone area, so Baronett probably was exposed to the idea almost as soon as it arrived here.

This F. Jay Haynes shot was probably taken in 1894 while the photographer was accompanying a winter survey of Yellowstone's wildlife. The photograph shows the Upper Alum Creek soldier cabin. The man on skis apparently is carrying in a chunk of log for firewood. Collecting firewood for backcountry patrol cabins must have been a never ending task for the soldiers.

National Park Service

Baronett was employed as a scout by the Yellowstone's civilian administration in the park's earliest days, often "hiring out" management of his bridge to free himself for the scouting work that must have better suited his adventurous personality. After the military assumed control of the park in August of 1886, Captain Moses Harris had requested authority to hire three civilian scouts. He was granted only one position, however, and that he bestowed on Baronett. Possibly indicating prior knowledge of the art of cross country skiing, Baronett accompanied Lieutenant Frederick Schwatka on his ill fated trip into the park in January of 1887. While Yellowstone Jack did not perform well on that trip, the cause may have been his reported ill health as well as his advancing age (he was then pushing 58). Even though he may not have been feeling well and was getting on in years, Baronett certainly would have passed on what he knew about skiing to the newly arrived troopers.

Ed Wilson, the "mountaineer assistant" who had accompanied famous photographer F. Jay Haynes on the latter's winter trip through the park in January 1887, was another who probably offered cross country skiing pointers to the newly arrived cavalry troopers. Remember, by early 1887 Wilson must have been somewhat proficient on skis, because he apparently skied solo from Mammoth to the Upper Geyser Basin after the Schwatka party had begun to disintegrate and Haynes had telephoned from Old Faithful to recruit the scout's assistance. His title of "mountaineer assistant" at the time of Schwatka-Haynes winter trip suggests that Captain Harris had circumvented his superiors' decision that he could hire only one scout when he had asked for three after his arrival in the park. It sure looks like Harris was employing at least one more de facto scout in addition to Jack Baronett, and that he had made Wilson's position acceptable to his higher ups simply by giving Wilson a different title. Wilson had been hired originally in his assistant position by the civilian authority that had preceded Captain Harris' assignment to the park, so maybe there was still enough civilian money on hand to keep Wilson employed. But playing with semantics as a technique of bureaucratic subterfuge has not been uncommon in Yellowstone's history, and it also could be argued that Captain Harris' need justified his means. Wilson actually did achieve the official title of scout when he replaced Jack Baronett, whose ill health forced him to resign the position the following summer.

At least some of the soldiers of the First Cavalry must have been quick learners. In mid April of 1887,

toward the end of the army's first winter in Yellowstone, Captain Harris was informed that a teamster who had been spending the winter in the Norris Hotel was probably trapping illegally in that area. In a clever move, Harris first disabled the telephone line between Mammoth and Norris so that there was no chance that the teamster, whose name was William James, could be tipped off. The captain then dispatched Sergeant John Swan with some enlisted men to ski the 22 miles to Norris and investigate. The soldiers made the trip under cover of darkness on the night of the 20th (they made it the whole way in just one night), and indeed found evidence of poaching in the form of traps and animals pelts. Teamster James frankly admitted his guilt, not just to trapping but also to poaching three elk at Canyon earlier in the winter. He also furnished the names of two accomplices, and added that the Norris Hotel winterkeeper Mr. Kelly, who had been so hospitable to the Schwatka and Haynes parties earlier in the winter, had been aware of his poaching. The soldiers arrested James and escorted him to Mammoth, where he was penalized by immediate expulsion from the park and forfeiture of the property he had been using in his illegal activities. James lost a rifle, his traps, his team of four horses, two sleds, four sets of harness, and various other smaller items and supplies. The skins of the animals he had poached were also taken from him. From frustrated poacher, James graduated to inept stagecoach robber when he and a confederate committed a holdup about one mile inside the park's north gate the following summer, on the Fourth of July. He bungled that, too, and wound up saddled with a hefty fine and sentenced to a year in prison for his troubles.

One of the passengers on the stagecoach held up by James and his accomplice was Judge John F. Lacey of Oskaloosa, Iowa. The robbers took a personal keepsake from Lacey that presumably had special value to the judge. Seven years later Lacey himself had graduated from a judge in Iowa to a representative in the United States Congress, apparently enjoying more success in his endeavors than James had enjoyed with his. As a representative in congress, Lacey found himself in a position to enact legislation that would have landmark importance in the protection of Yellowstone and other national parks. The legislation came in response to the actions of a different Yellowstone wrongdoer who was caught in the act early in 1894. Lacey's experience of being robbed at gunpoint in the park must have been a factor in his interest in the park, as well as in his desire to enact what came to be called the Lacey Act, which greatly enhanced legal

These five soldiers on ski patrol at Canyon appear to be a hard bitten, raw boned bunch. Note that most of the members of the detail are smoking. This shot must have been taken early in the winter as the snow depth is shallow — as evidenced by how much of the cart wheels and other accoutrements in the background are visible above the snow.

protection for Yellowstone and all other units in the national park system, up until and including the present time. There will be more about the Lacey Act later.

Ed Wilson had improved enough on his techniques to make a wide ranging ski patrol of the park the following winter. He took with him a sergeant from M Company, Charles Schroegler. The two men left Mammoth on February 12, 1888, traveled to Yancey's Hotel in Pleasant Valley near Tower, and then skied along Specimen Ridge and over Amethyst Mountain. From there they crossed the Mirror Plateau to Pelican Creek and then to Yellowstone Lake, and from there to Canyon, Norris and back to Mammoth. Evaluating that trip Captain Harris wrote "The hardships of an expedition of this character can only be realized by those who are acquainted with the winter aspect of the mountain solitudes into which these brave and hardy men ventured." Later that winter, in mid April, Wilson made another patrol across the snowy park, this time in the company of Uncle Billy Hofer. On this one Wilson and the indefatigable Hofer crossed the

Central Plateau, between the Yellowstone and Madison rivers, noting a herd of at least 100 buffalo somewhere in the area of Mary Mountain.

Scout Wilson was back out on his skis again the following winter, leaving Mammoth on February 10 on a trip to the geyser basins on the west side of the park. This time he took with him a corporal named William L. Boyce. They planned to begin their trip by touring the big geyser basins on the west side of the park and to continue from there to the thermal areas on the east side of Yellowstone Lake, which they wanted to check for bison. The February trip encountered bad weather and difficult snow conditions and the pair returned to Mammoth after a period of just ten days. They left again, however, on March 10, and did manage to make their intended circuit, but because of soft snow conditions they took so long to do so that Captain Harris wrote "some anxiety for their safety was felt." They did not see any bison on the east side of the lake, but they did see plenty of sign that the animals had been there earlier in the winter.

By now the patterns for these winter ski patrols were becoming established. The strategy behind regular patrols was, of course, to make frequent circuits through the park so that poachers would be deterred by the knowledge that troopers might appear anywhere at anytime. This was quite different from the reactive mode used by M Company during its first winter in Yellowstone, when soldiers ventured out from their base in Mammoth only in response to specific situations like the William James poaching case at Norris. And poaching was the army's chief concern when it began winter ski patrols. While there already were quite a few hotels and other properties in the park, most of these were looked after by winterkeepers employed by the private concessionaires, so the soldiers didn't have to be concerned so much with property violations. Indeed, winterkeepers had been part of the scene in wintry Yellowstone since at least 1880, so they predated the army by at least six years.

Security for wildlife was a different story. By 1886, European Americans had spent almost three hundred years in unbridled exploitation of wildlife and other natural resources in North America. While the traditions associated with that exploitation were deeply ingrained, Yellowstone National Park on the other hand had been in existence for less than 15 years, and the idea of Yellowstone as a wildlife refuge was quite a bit younger than that. Even in 1913, a full generation after the army's arrival in Yellowstone, the great naturalist William Hornaday observed that "Many men of the Great West...are afflicted with a desire to do as they please with the natural resources of that region." When people like William James and his confederates poached, or when the Norris Hotel winterkeeper Mr. Kelly turned a blind eye to their actions, they probably didn't think they were doing anything that was all that wrong. Similar exploitive attitudes toward wildlife and Yellowstone would have been prevalent among most local residents at the time and truth be told, probably among many of the First Cavalry Regiment's soldiers as well, at least among the rank and file. In the beginning, the soldiers probably exerted their efforts against poaching out of a sense of professional duty, and possibly out of a measure of piqued competitiveness. The sense of vested interest in place, as well as the sense of indignation when poachers violate the social contract that is the basis of preserves like Yellowstone, those were sources of motivation that probably came later. That said, it didn't take long for at least a certain cadre of soldiers and scouts to fully embrace Yellowstone for the special idea and the special place that it is and to devote themselves wholeheartedly to the preservation of its wonders, both animate and inanimate. In making the ideological transition from exploitation to preservation, they reflected the contemporary change in social attitudes toward nature and wildlife in general and toward Yellowstone in particular that occurred quite quickly after the park's creation.

When Yellowstone National Park was established in 1872, the primary reason behind its creation was its unique geothermals, and the secondary reason was the Grand Canyon and the great falls of the Yellowstone River. Wildlife was something of a throw in with the deal. In 1872 there were still large portions of the American West where wildlife was plentiful beyond belief. For example, then and now the principal debate about the abundance of the American buffalo, even as late as the 1870s, was an argument as to the number of millions there were. Just 14 years later, however, the buffalo had been all but exterminated, and many other species had suffered drastic population declines as well. More than just a reservation to protect its canyon and its geothermal features, Yellowstone was increasingly valued as a wildlife preserve. Because of the near elimination of bison elsewhere, and the fact that a few hundred were hanging on in the most remote sections of the park, the species was viewed with special concern from the time the army first arrived in the new park. Actually, concern for Yellowstone's bison was responsible as much as anything for the ski patrols initiated by the cavalry in the early days of their occupation of the park.

There is little question that bison have inhabited what is now Yellowstone National Park for a very long time. Their ancestors probably colonized the area shortly after the ice melted off the Yellowstone Plateau at the end of the Pinedale Glaciation, and their kind have endured here until the present. Paleontological and archeological finds support this view, as do the written records of many of those who traveled through the Yellowstone area in early historic times. The Yellowstone herd had been spared the mass slaughter of the 1870s and early 1880s that had eliminated the vast bison herds of the Great Plains — the park animals fortunately were too remote, lived in a habitat with more cover than the plains, and were too few in number to attract much attention from the rapacious hide hunters who were more interested in quantity rather than quality of raw skins. At the height of the trade in raw skins, in the early 1870s, the price per hide sank as low as $1.25. But by the late 1880s, because of the gross diminution of the herds and the desire by the wealthy to own a token of a species which many thought was on the fast track to extinction, the price of a quality hide suitable for mounting by a taxidermist ranged between $400.00 and $1,000.00. This estimate was taken from the 1891 Yellowstone superintendent's report, and especially when you consider the time period, amounted to more than enough money to encourage poachers to violate the law and to make the effort required to access the remaining Yellowstone bison in their remote haunts.

Other military records from the late 1800s offer further glimpses into the plight of Yellowstone's buffalo, as well as the army's measures to protect them. Biologists are in agreement that the bison that originally inhabited Yellowstone were the mountain variety. As such, they tended to spend much of their time in secluded forest habitats where they enjoyed a measure of security over what their much more numerous brethren had on the open plains. Nonetheless, government estimates of Yellowstone's bison population, gleaned mostly from winter ski patrols, trace a depressing decline in numbers from the time the army first arrived until 1902. That year the park herd bottomed out when only 23 of the animals were counted, although the people who did the counting admitted that there could have been at least that many more of the animals that they had not seen. Describing the situation the very next year, in 1903, Yellowstone scout Peter Holt wrote, "All that is left of the once mighty herds that roamed the plains are perhaps twenty-five, which have taken refuge in the wildest and most inaccessible part of the Rocky Mountains set aside as a national park. They are so extremely shy that they can only be seen in winter, and only by those able to penetrate to their mountain fastness on skis.... It may thus be seen how difficult it is to keep any track of these animals — to learn their exact number and what the increase or decrease has been during the year."

In spite of the tutelage of scouts like Ed Wilson and Jack Baronett, dispatching ski patrols to protect the buffalo and other wildlife remained a challenge for the cavalry. Baronett's age and Wilson's suicide took them out of the picture in pretty short order, and in general

there were never enough scouts with the necessary qualifications, those qualifications being knowledge of the Yellowstone country, ability to ski, and the desire to serve. Probably an even bigger problem was the turnover among the ranks of the soldiers themselves. Many units served in the park for a period of only three years. Captain Moses Harris and his M Company, for example, arrived in Yellowstone in 1886 and transferred out in 1889. Under this rotational strategy, soldiers were just starting to learn the country, and more importantly were starting to make progress

National Park Service

Arriving at a way station to find it buried in snow must have been a fairly common occurrence for U.S. Cavalry troopers on ski patrol.

in the art of cross country skiing, when they were withdrawn from the park. The army bureaucratically compounded this problem by rotating entire units in and out at the same time, so that there was no continuity of lore among individual veterans (other than the small core of civilian scouts) who in turn could pass on what they had learned to newcomers.

Additionally, in common with soldiers of almost any era the soldiers of the late 19th century era tended to be from undereducated and underprivileged backgrounds, and ended up in the army because there weren't that many other options open to them. Once in the army, the poor fellows had to go where they were sent, and so wound up in Yellowstone by way of military caprice rather than by personal choice. As an old timer in Yellowstone once said, "There's them that's made for this country and there's them that ain't."

Nevertheless, when the famous western artist Frederic Remington visited the park in 1893, just seven

A famous photo of Scout Felix Burgess and others escorting the infamous poacher Ed Howell from where he was captured in Pelican Valley to park headquarters at Mammoth Hot Springs. Yellowstone photographer F. Jay Haynes shot this picture at Norris in March of 1894. The Howell case was publicized nationally, and led to congressional legislation that greatly strengthened protective powers for park managers.

years after the army's initial appearance on the Yellowstone scene, he was able to write:

"In winter the snow covers the ground to a great depth.... The rounds of the Park are then made by mounting the cavalry on the ski, or Norwegian snowshoe [sic], and with its aid men travel the desolate snow-clad [sic] wilderness from one 'shack' to another. Small squads of three or four men are quartered in these remote recesses of the savage mountains, and remain for eight months on a stretch. The camps are provisioned for the arctic siege, and what is stranger yet is that the soldiers rather like it, and freely apply for this detached service... it shows good spirit on the part of the enlisted men. They are dressed in fur caps, California blanket coats, leggings, and moccasins — a strange uniform for the cavalryman...."

From Remington's take on things, by 1893 it sounds like the cavalry had figured out the winter patrol business to a great extent, even down to an appropriate ensemble of clothing. Then just a few years later another writer observed that the army's Yellowstone ski patrollers faced many challenges, "but the spirit that has carried these same troopers to victory in Cuba and Guam, here also comes to the fore, and the work, whatever it may be, is done, and done as all work in the army is, thoroughly." It seems that the army was doing well enough, undoubtedly with help from their hired scouts.

The winter after Remington's visit they did well enough, again with the help of one of their scouts, to capture one of the most notorious poachers in the history of Yellowstone. Edgar Howell had entered the park through the northeast entrance early in the winter of 1893-1894 in the company of a partner. Howell and his sidekick had passed by the Soda Butte soldier station in the night on their way into the park, and thereby had naturally elicited suspicion from the troopers on duty there. West of Soda Butte the shady pair, who were towing a toboggan behind them as they shuffled along on skis, had branched off to the south of the main trail through Lamar Valley and had crossed Specimen Ridge. Their route then took them up and over the Mirror Plateau and down to Astringent Creek, a tributary flowing into Pelican Creek from the north. There they were close to the wintering range of one of the largest segments of the imperiled

Yellowstone bison herd, then estimated to total about 400 head, and there the two miscreants set up winter camp with the intention of killing all the buffalo they could. Their plan was then to cache the "scalps," or what today we would call the mountable capes off the animals' heads and necks, in trees where they would be safe from scavengers until the men could return with pack horses to retrieve their trophies, after the snow had melted in the spring. According to an army officer who was to become involved in the Howell case, the scalps would fetch between $100 and $300 apiece once they had been smuggled out of the park.

Shortly after Howell and his partner, whose name was Noble, had established their camp on Astringent Creek the two men had a set to for some reason, and the partner left and returned to Cooke City. But Ed Howell soon proved that he didn't need any help to kill buffalo — he would later boast that he had killed 80 of the wintering animals in Pelican Valley before his apprehension. If Howell's brag was correct, and if the army's estimate of the total bison population was accurate, that means that just this one poacher was responsible for the destruction of 20% of Yellowstone's herd in just one winter.

The first step in Howell's apprehension, other than the original suspicion he and his partner had brought on themselves with their middle-of-the-night passage through the Soda Butte and Lamar valleys, was made by an army ski patrol that had been sent out to check on the buffalo to the east of the Yellowstone River and Yellowstone Lake. Their route took them into Pelican Valley, where they noticed some suspicious toboggan tracks. It didn't take long for someone in the cavalry to make the association between the tracks and Howell's sneaky entrance into the park earlier that winter, so in early March an army detachment under Captain G.L. Scott was sent from Mammoth to Lake Hotel, there to set up a base of operations to find out what was going on in Pelican Valley. From the hotel, which was then only three years old, two men in the detachment were dispatched to investigate the toboggan tracks more fully. The two men were Scout Felix Burgess, who was a hardened veteran of the Indian wars in the Southwest, and a sergeant whose last name was Troike. Burgess and Troike had little trouble finding Howell's camp, in which there was a tepee, six stashed buffalo heads, and some other items related to the business of poaching. While still looking around the poacher's camp the investigators heard six gun shots in the distance. By following the sound of the shots they located Howell himself, out in Pelican Valley with his dog and five freshly killed bison.

When Burgess and Troike spotted him, Howell was engaged in severing the head from one of the downed buffalo. While the poacher was thus occupied, the scout and the sergeant in "an act of bravery that deserved especial mention and recognition," raced across 400 yards of open snowscape in Pelican Valley to close the distance between themselves and the poacher. Burgess and Troike were lucky as well as brave---the wind was so strong and noisy that neither Howell nor his dog heard them coming until the scout, who apparently had surged ahead of the sergeant, announced his presence from a distance of 15 or 20 feet. The close approach was key, since Burgess and Troike had only one .38 caliber army revolver between them, while Howell was armed with a repeating rifle with much longer range. And after Howell's arrest, the poacher declared that Burgess never would have taken him if he had seen the scout coming at a distance. While some interpreters think that meant that Howell would have shot it out, the poacher actually clarified himself a bit later by saying that he meant he would have jumped on his skis and made a run for it, and that "he could travel as far in a day on those shoes [which were crude, cobbled together affairs] as any man in the party could with any other pair...." As it was, Howell recognized his situation for the disadvantageous one that it was, and gave up without resistance. "I see I was subjec' to the drop, so I let go my knife and came along," as Howell himself put it.

In spite of Howell's bravado in saying that he never would have been captured if he had seen Burgess in time, once arrested he apparently cooperated fully and even seemed to enjoy some aspects of his captivity. Burgess and Troike escorted him out of Pelican Valley, first going by way of Lake Hotel and then stopping at other way stations along the road to park headquarters at Mammoth. From Lake Hotel on their first night out of the wilds of Pelican Valley, news of Howell's arrest was telephoned to Captain George Anderson, then acting as superintendent of the park. The next stop was at the Canyon Hotel, where the group spent a night and Howell ate 24 pancakes for breakfast the next morning. It would seem safe to say that Howell welcomed the opportunity to vary his diet, which out in the snowy backcountry probably had been mostly if not wholly restricted to the meat of the animals he had poached. And Howell was not that concerned with the fact that he had been caught. In response to questioning, Howell answered "Yes, I am going to take a little walk up to the Post [meaning park headquarters at Mammoth], but I don't think

I'll be there long.... I may go back into the Park again, later on, and I may not."

Even though Howell cooperated with them, Burgess and Howell felt they had their hands full in shepherding their prisoner, so they did not haul any of the poacher's bison heads out of Pelican Valley as they ideally would like to have done. Some of the other soldiers involved in the operation must have gone out to the valley a short time later and retrieved the heads, however, because at least some of Howell's ill gotten trophies later appeared at park headquarters at Mammoth. At least there is a photograph that purports to show the mounted heads of some of the bison killed by Howell and later retrieved and preserved by the army, and there is a record of the trophies being given to high ranking officers of the army as well as to some civilian figures who were considered sufficiently important. It is interesting that the same bureaucrats who were so quick to criticize the morals of wealthy individuals who wanted to collect bison parts in the interest of owning a piece of the Old West were just as quick to appropriate such a remembrance for themselves when the opportunity presented itself. Whoever retrieved the "scalps" from Pelican Valley must have done so promptly after Howell's arrest, before the heads were destroyed by scavengers.

Now, it so happened that at the time of Howell's arrest a correspondent named Emerson Hough from the conservation magazine Field and Stream was on assignment in the park. Ostensibly, Hough was there to replicate the wildlife survey of the park done in 1887 by Billy Hofer. Hofer was involved this time, too, to serve as guide and consultant to Hough; the magazine correspondent especially needed Hofer's instruction in the art of cross country skiing. Photographer F. Jay Haynes was involved as well, to go along on the trip and photograph whatever the survey might find. On the night that Scout Burgess and Sergeant Troike returned with prisoner Howell to Lake Hotel, and the news was telephoned to park headquarters, it further happened that correspondent Hough was visiting as a guest in the home of Captain and Park Superintendent George Anderson. If things hadn't been bureaucratically orchestrated up until that point, it certainly appears that they were from then on.

After receiving the news of Howell's capture, Captain Anderson was described as "positively jubilant through every inch of his 6ft. 2in. of muscular and military humanity. He couldn't sit still, he was so glad." Next it was arranged, presumably by Anderson or his subordinates, for the outbound Hough party to meet with the inbound Scout Burgess and Sergeant

Troike and their prisoner at Norris. At Norris F. Jay Haynes photographed Howell and his captors, and Hough interviewed both Burgess and Howell. Hough would publish the story of Howell's poaching and his capture as part of a series of articles he wrote about his winter tour through the park for Forest & Stream — Hough actually sent the text of his article about the Howell affair with Burgess and Troike to Mammoth, as Hough himself continued on south with Billy Hofer on their survey of wintering wildlife in the park.

Hough's article about Howell was telegraphed from park headquarters at Mammoth to the editor of Field and Stream, who was the passionate and well connected conservationist George Bird Grinnell. Grinnell not only circulated the story of Howell's escapades and arrest nationally in his magazine, he also recruited other influential people to travel with him to Washington D.C., there to lobby with Congress for stronger laws and harsher punishments for crimes in national parks, especially for crimes against wildlife. Grinnell and his circle of conservationists found a receptive ear for their concerns in the person of Representative John Lacey of Iowa. Lacey, it may be recalled, was the same John Lacey who had been victimized by poacher-turned-stagecoach-robber William James on the road between Gardiner and Mammoth in July of 1887. In response to the appeals made by Grinnell and his associates, Lacey introduced H.R. 6442, which was named for its sponsor and is still known as The Lacey Act. Notable for its longevity, the act is still a principal tool of law enforcement in national parks today. The entire chain of events that led to the bill's creation progressed with remarkable dispatch, and it was less than two weeks after Burgess and Troike heard Howell's six shots that killed those five bison in remote Pelican Valley when Representative Lacey introduced his bill in the nation's capitol. The bill continued to move expeditiously through the legislative process and was passed on May 7, 1894.

Strengthened penalties were essential to preserving Yellowstone's dwindling bison herd and other wildlife. Before the Lacey Act, the only penalties the U.S. Army could invoke against poachers and other wrongdoers were confiscation of equipment employed in the commission of the crime and expulsion from the park for offenders. As one park official put it, "Confiscation of the outfit, under existing regulations, has but little effect, as the outfit is generally worthless." Howell again serves as a good example. His "outfit" consisted of his gun, an axe, some crudely cobbled together skis, a home made toboggan, and not much more. Howell didn't even have shoes or boots, for gosh sakes, when he was out in wintry Pelican Valley. He just clothed his feet in a pair of indifferent socks, and then inserted them into some old feed sacks he had nailed to his skis when he went skiing. The total value of his kit was put at $26.75, against which he stood to make several thousand dollars if he had pulled off his poaching season as he had planned. Parenthetically, it seems like Howell could have at least fashioned some sort of moccasins out of buffalo hide while he was passing those long winter nights in his tepee along Astringent Creek. Anything would have better than thin socks in the snow in that country.

Expulsion from the park didn't amount to much, either, as the army had no legal provisions for a continuation of a ban from the park after an offender had been kicked out. As Howell had said after his arrest, "I may go back into the Park again, later on, and I may not." But now the Lacey Act, while preserving the power of the government to confiscate equipment and to expel offenders from the park, provided for hefty fines for lawbreaking, as well as allowing for substantial prison sentences. The act was big part of part of the reason that the Yellowstone buffalo herd did survive in the wild from prehistoric times until the present, the only herd with that profound distinction anywhere in the United States.

The army continued their ski patrols for their entire tenure in Yellowstone. To house their men along the trail, a total of 19 patrol cabins were built during the 1890s. The cabins, which at the time were referred to as "snowshoe cabins," were spaced around the park roughly a day's ski apart and improved the effectiveness of patrol by reducing the amount of equipment that soldiers had to carry. The cabins were in addition to the existing soldier stations, which primarily were located at the points of principal interest in the park. Troopers on winter patrol also used the slightly more commodious stations when their patrol routes allowed.

Even with the protection from the elements afforded by the army stations and the snowshoe cabins, at least seven soldiers died from avalanches or freezing while on winter patrol. These deaths also occurred in spite of various protocols that the army bureaucracy put in place to protect the welfare of its men, such as a stipulation that patrols could not be conducted alone, and another that prescribed appropriate winter clothing to be worn while out on the trail. The first of the army men who died from the wintry elements was Private Andrew Preiber, who collapsed on the road between Gardiner and Mammoth on March 14, 1893. The next was Private David J. Matthews, who disap-

peared on March 14, 1894 while en route from Riverside soldier station (near today's West Yellowstone) to another station in the Lower Geyser Basin. His body was not found for more than a year, and there was considerable contemporary suspicion that Matthews had been killed by poachers. No real evidence to that effect was ever found, however, and the most likely cause of his demise was disorientation and exposure to the frigid elements.

The next soldier to die was John W.H. Davis, who died on December 14, 1897 along the north shore of Yellowstone Lake. Davis and his partner, a Private Murphy, had left Lake Hotel for West Thumb that morning, but Murphy had been unable to continue because of the intensely cold weather. Davis had carried on alone after Murphy had turned back, but had made it only about another two miles before he succumbed to weather that was probably colder than 35 below zero. Scout Billy Hofer, who seems to have been nearly omnipresent in Yellowstone in those days, commented that it seemed "almost impossible for a man to lose his life in such a way in that country as there is any quantity of dry wood and timber all along the road." But Davis had indeed died, and the evacuation of his frozen corpse to Mammoth required heroic efforts from several of his still living mates.

A corporal in the cavalry, Christ H. Martin, died in an avalanche along the Gallatin River in the northwestern corner of Yellowstone on February 17, 1904. Martin and another corporal had left the Gallatin soldier station at the mouth of Specimen Creek in the morning, bound for the station at Riverside. In spite of an admonition from a local prospector to avoid a certain avalanche-prone slope, the two soldiers skied into the danger zone at the foot of the slope and the disturbance of their passing is likely what triggered the slide that buried Martin. In spite of the efforts of his companion, who had survived by grasping a tree while being carried along by the river of snow, and the subsequent efforts of a number of other soldiers, Martin's body was not recovered until April 16.

Another soldier became sickened at South Entrance and was being escorted by some of his fellows to Mammoth for medical care when he died at West Thumb in April of 1904. Private Richard R. Hurley died from some combination of his illness and the cold after being left alone in a station at Thumb when his buddies went out on patrol. One version of Hurley's demise has it that his body was found in a position that indicated he had been unsuccessfully attempting to kindle a fire in the station's stove when he succumbed. Again, the evacuation of his body became a Yellowstone epic, one remembered for the rest of the lives of those who participated in the operation.

Private Presley H. Vance died in Elk Park on October 16, 1908. Alcohol was heavily involved in his death, and though his was not technically a winter death because he died while on horse patrol, he did die by freezing. Vance froze to death after falling off his horse, and he died in spite of being in the company of as many as three other soldiers. Unfortunately for Vance, all of his companions were also drunk and apparently in no shape to save him.

The penultimate death involving a winter traveler in the army era was that of Bill "Scout" Jones, who died late in the year 1910. Described as an "old time scout and hunter," Jones nonetheless became disoriented while hauling a load of supplies in a blizzard along the north boundary of the park. Epilepsy may have been a contributing factor, but Jones' body was found about three miles away from the mining town of Jardine, Montana, just outside Yellowstone's boundary. Exposure was presumed to be the cause of his death, as his body was not found until nine months after his disappearance, and in all probability any evidence that might have explained the circumstances surrounding Jones' death had weathered away by the time his body was discovered.

The last winter-related death of a military man came very near the end of the army's time in Yellowstone. Lieutenant Joseph McDonald died in an improbable snow slide near Cleopatra Terrace at Mammoth Hot Springs on January 9, 1916. On the afternoon of that date, which was a Sunday, McDonald and three others were skiing around the hot spring terraces above park headquarters when they were caught in a snow slide. Such an eventuality is unlikely at Mammoth, as the area is low in elevation relative to most of Yellowstone and consequently does not receive nearly as much snowfall as most of the rest of the park. Nonetheless, the party was struck by the slide and all but one of its members were buried. The one not buried was able to extricate two of the victims in short order, but McDonald could not be located immediately. Help arrived from the headquarters area below, and with the extra hands McDonald was uncovered after about 45 minutes of being buried face down in the snow, but he never regained consciousness and died about two hours later. Joe McDonald was well liked and engaged to be married at the time of his death, so his death hit hard and greatly saddened the Mammoth community.

Isolation was another problem for the patrolling soldiers. The troopers were often confined to the stations and cramped snowshoe cabins along their patrol routes for months at a time. Their winter work was exhausting---one officer's description of the duty was that "the hardships are inconceivable"---as well as dangerous. They endured the winter season with only a small company of other males for companionship, and winter nights in Yellowstone were long and dark.

The most lethal manifestation of cabin fever occurred at the Sylvan Pass soldier station during the winter of 1911-1912. That winter one sergeant and four privates were stationed there. As the winter progressed a deadly split evolved between the NCO, whose name was Clarence Britton, and one of the privates, whose name was Frank Cunningham. Private Cunningham was reportedly a large and imposing man, and the other privates invariably sided with him when the frequent disputes arose with Sergeant Britton. All five collectively "snarled and quarreled." There was a working telephone that connected their station to headquarters at Mammoth, but for whatever reason none of the five soldiers ever used it. Perhaps they did not want to communicate to anyone just how bad things had gotten at the Sylvan Pass station, which was located not on Sylvan Pass itself but rather at the site of today's East Entrance, about 55 miles west of the town of Cody, Wyoming.

Things deteriorated between Sergeant Britton and Private Cunningham and his supporters until one day in late March, when Britton departed the station on ski patrol but made it only a short distance before breaking a ski pole. When he returned to the station to replace the broken pole, he walked in on the four privates as they were engaged in a conversation about their sergeant that was less than complimentary. Heated exchanges and masculine challenges led to Cunningham making a rush at the sergeant, who quickly pulled his revolver and shot the private between the eyes, killing him instantly. Another private named Frank Carrol was advancing toward Britton just behind Cunningham, and a second shot from the sergeant hit him in the arm and nearly severed a large artery. A timely tourniquet saved Carrol's life. Subsequent legal actions cleared Sergeant Britton on the grounds of self defense, and sentenced the three surviving privates to prison for mutiny for periods of two years for the two men who did not attack the NCO and three years for Carrol, who did attack and received a bullet in the arm as a prelude to his imprisonment. Yes, winter nights in Yellowstone were long and dark.

We can think back and envision with certainty that practically all of the United States Cavalry troops who came to Yellowstone arrived here not by their own personal choice but rather by the chance of military assignment. Again by chance, some of the soldiers found the park to their liking, a good fit for their personalities and abilities. Inevitably most did not. Undoubtedly these disparities were heightened by the extremes of Yellowstone's winter. We can further imagine what it would have been like for the individual soldier out on his skis, his head enshrouded in the vapor from his own breath, feeling the sting of snow crystals on his face and the overpowering presence of the cold. In the absence of wind, we can think of him sensing the immutable weight of the snowy silence. At other times we can imagine him shuffling through ground blizzards in places like Hayden Valley, or watching columns of twirling snow out on the ice of Yellowstone Lake that put him in mind of dust devils he had seen in the desert southwest, only these swirling devils were made of snow. We can imagine him looking up at ominous clouds blowing overhead, or feeling impending darkness closing in on him through the endless ranks of unmoving trees, while he still had miles to go before he arrived at the next patrol cabin or soldier station.

In spite of army protocols forbidding solitary travel, he probably found himself out alone quite often. Even with a companion he probably spent most of his time alone in his head, listening to the repetitive scratch of his skis on the snow as he shoved them ahead one after another, step and step, time after time, wondering how deep the snow was underfoot, how dark it would be before he got to where he was going, how cold the cabin would be when he finally did get there, how many days it would be before he could have a whiskey. Feeling the cramps in his feet and the stiffness in his fingers and enveloped by great wind and blowing snow and miles and miles of uninhabited forest, a man could be thrilled with exultation or concussed with despair depending on his makeup and mood, and the two emotional extremes could strike the same man alternately and be separated by only a few moments in time. A trooper with the moxie of a Billy Hofer could shout with exhilaration at the sight of huge snow covered mountains, while a private from Arkansas or Georgia, or for that matter a new recruit from Italy or Ireland, could look at the same wintry landscape and be cowed, and to dread that he would never get out of those mountains and that he might well die there.

Once in the cabin, a man would be sheltered by rude walls and low slung roof and gratefully warmed by the fire in the stove. He would be fed and refreshed with army bacon and coffee, but he might feel holed up and small, like a mouse living in the wall of the barracks back at post. Outside the tiny shelter loomed the immensity of darkness and distance, and there was always the deep silence and the unrelenting cold, cold that became ever more inconceivable as the night deepened. In the smoke that leaked from the stove and wafted around his head might be thoughts of mothers and girls, and memories of old homes left behind and painful thoughts of new homes never found. Sleep might have brought restless dreams of splashing hot springs and tremendous clouds of geothermal steam billowing into frigid air. The next day would begin with the hard labor of chopping wood at the cabin, maybe getting the mind together enough to work civilly with another soldier, and then setting off on those long and clumsy skis again, again to deal with the blinding light on the snow and the wind sighing through pine needles and the crushing thoughts inside a lonely man's head. It must have been a hard and lonely life.

© Jeff Henry

Jack Richard Collection, Buffalo Bill Historical Center

Two rangers leave the Lake Hotel area on ski patrol across the ice of Yellowstone Lake in early March 1969. It appears they are heading for the Thorofare country, some forty miles distant.

IX

The Rangers

"Sliding the boundary trails from station to snowshoe cabin and back again, that poachers might be kept out and game protected."

Early season snowstorm along the Firehole River.

It took the United States Army 28 years to realize that its program of rotating entire units of cavalry into and out of Yellowstone at the same time was not the best idea. With the fairly short stay that each unit had in the park there was little continuity, and the majority of individual troopers who were more or less randomly assigned to the park were unsuited to the duty. Assignment to Yellowstone didn't work that well from the military point of view, either. Duty in the park tended to fragment units, as small groups of men were scattered at the different stations around the park and were removed from centralized command. In a larger sense, entire units were taken away from their home bases and were collectively removed from command structure, and during the time they were stationed in Yellowstone they were absent from training programs, which were more likely to be conducted at bona fide military posts.

Recognition of these problems in 1914 led to the army adopting a system where individual soldiers were drawn on a merit basis for assignment to Yellowstone from a total of nine different cavalry regiments. The key to this system was that men volunteered for service in the park, and consequently they tended to be much better suited to the task than the personnel who had been bureaucratically assigned under the earlier scheme. At the same time that the army was instituting this more sensible program there were political machinations going on both in military and civilian realms to create a bureau for national parks, and to relieve the military of its park duties altogether and turn protection and other tasks over to a civilian work force.

The first people employed in Yellowstone who could be considered park rangers were hired in the summer of 1915. They were a group of four, and the principal reason they were hired was to collect entry fees from automobiles entering the park. That year marked the first time that cars were legally allowed to enter Yellowstone, and one reason they were admitted is that it was thought that the entrance fees they were charged could be used to fund park operations. Cars were not admitted to Yellowstone until August 1915, so the four seasonal employees hired to collect entrance fees from them had short seasons.

In the autumn of that year the park hired two more seasonal rangers, these to assist in predator control. At the time Yellowstone was in the midst of a prolonged campaign to protect animals that had been judged to be "good," mainly herbivores, by killing off species that had been judged to be "bad," which were mostly large carnivores. Hiring on to work with wildlife was indicative of much of the work that rangers would be assigned to do after the creation of the National Park Service.

Management authority of Yellowstone National Park was formally transferred from the army to the newly created National Park Service on September 30,

Two Yellowstone National Park rangers, thought to be the legendary duo Harry Trischman (left) and Joe Douglas, head out of Mammoth to patrol the park on skis. National Park Service archives attribute a 1920s date to the photograph and the rangers' garb appears to confirm the date. Their lack of standardized uniforms stands in strong contrast to the apparel of present-day rangers.

1916. The new agency was fortunate to have the pool of soldiers who had volunteered for duty in the park to draw on for its initial contingent of rangers. In the words of Horace Albright, one of pioneers of the NPS, the agreement between the army and the service arranged for "the release of a number of sergeants and corporals who had had such experience in leadership and had shown real interest in Yellowstone Park, these men to be appointed park rangers. Other rangers were to be recruited from stage drivers, scouts who were on duty to help the soldiers (there were only four or five of them) etc." With regard to infrastructure, Albright added that "Fort Yellowstone with all its buildings, including a fully equipped hospital, many horses, wagons, etc. were to be transferred [as well]."

Albright's smooth verbiage indicates that he and his boss, Stephen Mather, thought they had things all figured out. But in reality the transition was not as smooth as the verbiage. Another round of political jockeying ended with the new park service being left without funding, and the new ranger force was disbanded on June 30, 1917. Nor was this the only regression, as the army was recalled to take over man-

agement of the park one more time. This time around the army's handling of the park was even shakier than before. For one thing, probably all involved realized that the military's tenure in the park this time was indeed temporary. A bigger factor was that the United States by then had entered The Great War, and the best the army had, both in manpower and in other resources, was being sent to Europe. Troops stationed in the national park on this go around appear to have been decidedly second string. The National Park Service received renewed funding for the fiscal year beginning on July 1, 1918, and at that point began to reconstitute their original ranger force. Again the new agency was fortunate in that a basic core of ten of the original rangers had been kept on as scouts for the army, and these men were on location and available for rehire as rangers.

Chief among this group of ten was Jim McBride. Born in 1864, McBride was possibly one of the last players in Yellowstone who could truly be considered a frontiersman. The best interpretation is that he arrived in the park in the mid 1880s. He may have been a private in the army stationed in the Upper Geyser

Basin in 1886, which if true means he came to Yellowstone with Captain Moses Harris' first contingent of U.S. Cavalry. He was definitely employed as a scout for the army by 1900, and he was chief of scouts by 1914. Somewhere along the way he befriended Theodore Roosevelt, probably on or around Roosevelt's ranch near Medora, North Dakota. McBride guided Roosevelt on the latter's 1903 trip through Yellowstone, and one source has McBride making the original suggestion to construct an arch at the North Entrance to the park. Roosevelt definitely called McBride to the speaker's platform for special recognition when the president dedicated the Roosevelt Arch in 1903. Jim McBride is further distinguished as having been named the first chief ranger in Yellowstone, a title he held from 1918 until 1922. A contemporary described McBride thusly: "A quiet man, big and silent like his habitat, with something of the free wildness of his friends [the wild animals]. Mostly in his patrol he sticks to the trails and, day and night, the year 'round, rides his lonely way looking for poachers...observing the wild things and their doings and welfare." Possibly too well adapted to the frontier and to riding the silent trails, McBride apparently had trouble adjusting to more modern conditions in Yellowstone, especially with regard to motor vehicles, and he was reassigned from the chief ranger position to wildlife management after a fairly brief tenure.

Another storied character hired on as one of Yellowstone's original rangers was Harry Trischman. He was born in 1886 at Fort Custer, Montana, the same military post that had furnished the first cavalry unit sent to protect Yellowstone that very same year. Trischman first moved to the park when his father was hired as post carpenter for Fort Yellowstone in 1899. In one of the most unspeakable tragedies in Yellowstone's history, Trischman's mother had gone homicidally insane shortly after the family's arrival here, and had cut the throat of Harry's five year old brother, Joseph. Margaret Trischman killed her younger son in front of Harry and his two sisters, and then continuing with her madness, tried to turn the knife on the other three children. Harry and his sisters escaped to a neighbor's house at Mammoth and so survived, but a few days later his mother committed suicide by

National Park Service

In Yellowstone National Park archives this photo carries the notation "Some of the Difficulties of Winter Travel on the South Entrance Road." The principle difficulty is, of course, the deep and powdery snow, for which that part of Yellowstone is so deservedly known.

jumping from a train into the Yellowstone River while en route to a hospital for the insane. In spite of a sustained effort by many searchers, her body was never found.

Harry Trischman and his sisters overcame their childhood trauma and managed to construct long careers in Yellowstone. The sisters, Anna and Elizabeth, ran a successful curio store and soda fountain at Mam-

A ranger in front of the Crystal Springs patrol cabin on January 17, 1936. Note the long skis parked in front of the cabin.

Rangers and winterkeepers returning to Canyon after evacuating an appendicitis-stricken winterkeeper named Winlare from Lake Hotel to Mammoth, 1939.

Rangers measuring awesome snow depths at the Bechler Ranger Station in February 1933.

Three rangers in a thermal area along the Firehole River just upstream from the Old Faithful complex, an area once known as the "Bears Playground." Additional archived photos of these men document a long ski tour of the park they completed in February and March, 1930.

moth for their entire adult lives, not giving up the enterprise until 1953. For his part, Harry began working for the army in Yellowstone in 1907, became a scout in 1909, and a ranger in 1916. In later years he worked his way up to assistant chief ranger, and also was employed as chief buffalo keeper. He was described as a "man of tremendous physical strength," an attribute that helped him continue ranger work until he was 59 years old. Trischman has often been noted for the poignant entry he left in the log of the Crevice backcountry patrol cabin just before his retirement. Thinking ahead to his imminent departure from the park, he wrote simply, "They won't let me sleep in their cabins any more." Clearly, Trischman had been cut out for the job, as had James McBride and many of their contemporaries.

Being cut out for the job and having personally chosen the duty made the new rangers quite different, of course, from the soldiers during the army's regime. As the venerable Aubrey Haines, first dean of Yellowstone historians described them, the new force of park rangers were "practical men, with less education and more experience than their present-day counterparts," and that "they shared an esprit de corps that was a Yellowstone trait. It came in part from the scouts and their dependence on personal competence, appearing in the ranger force as pride in an ability to do whatever was required...."

One of the more important things required in winter, of course, was the continuation of the ski patrols pioneered by the army and developed in part by some of the same men who had made the transition from soldiering and scouting to rangering. As a newspaper article from the time described their winter work, "on bitter nights last winter [in Yellowstone], around many a hearth, there was thought for the lonely...men on ski patrol. Sliding the boundary trails from station to snowshoe cabin and back again, that poachers might be kept out and game protected...."

By the time the army departed and the National Park Service rangers arrived on the scene, the buffalo population had recovered markedly and the animals were no longer in dire danger of extinction. No other species in Yellowstone were in danger of extinction from poaching, either, but poaching patrols continued as a matter of principal, a sort of hold-the-line-at-water's-edge mentality on the part of the new rangers. The rangers used the same patrol routes and the same patrol cabins as had the soldiers before them, and of course they had to cope with the same challenges from natural elements and social isolation.

More than just patrolling to protect wildlife from poachers, the new Yellowstone rangers spent a good deal of their time directly managing the animals in their charge. In 1902, when the park's bison population reached its nadir, it was decided that the only sure way to save the species was to supplement the wild population with some new stock, and to actively manage the new animals with ranching principles. To this end, three bull bison were brought from Charles Goodnight's captive herd in Texas, and 18 cows were procured from dude rancher Howard Eaton, who in turn had established his herd with stock from the Pablo-Allard captive herd in western Montana. This original stock was supplemented with four calves captured from the remaining wild herd in the park. This so-called tame herd reproduced rapidly from the original 25 members and by 1918, when the National Park Service permanently took over the administration of Yellowstone, they officially numbered 385 animals.

In the beginning, the tame herd was penned at Mammoth, where they were displayed for the viewing pleasure of the visiting public. The herd soon outgrew its Mammoth quarters, however, and in 1906 most of the bison were moved to a site selected near the mouth of Rose Creek in Lamar River Valley. There, at what came to be known as the Buffalo Ranch, the bison were managed very much like domestic livestock. Techniques employed at various times included inoculations against disease, segregating the buffalo by gender, bottle feeding the calves after first separating them from their mothers, and castration of bulls judged to be of lesser quality and therefore unfit to serve as sires. In the beginning the animals were always contained within fences, or at least closely shepherded during the day and returned to their corrals at night. Ostensibly this was to protect them from poachers, but their handlers also wanted to keep them under a watchful eye. Additionally, large tracts of land in Lamar Valley and elsewhere were first cleared of native vegetation and then irrigated to grow considerable quantities of hay, which was used to feed the animals during the winter. The intensity of ranching efforts gradually relaxed as time went by, and the tame herd began to mingle with the wild herd sometime during the 1920s, but supplemental feeding of bison continued to varying extents until 1952. By the nature of the climate in Yellowstone, a great deal of the most dramatic work at the Buffalo Ranch took place during the winter.

By sometime around 1915 the tame herd was allowed to range more freely away from the ranch. A

Bison congregate along a feeding line of hay, strewn by the buffalo keepers at Lamar Buffalo Ranch in March 1932. This flat is on the north side of the Lamar River, just across the Northeast Entrance Road from today's Lamar Ranger Station and the Yellowstone Institute's educational complex.

drift fence was soon erected across the lower end of Lamar Valley and it kept the animals from moving in that direction, so for the most part the animals ranged upriver and eventually began using the slopes of the Absaroka Mountains around the head of Lamar River as their summer range. From these rather distant summer ranges it was thought that the buffalo had to be driven back to the Buffalo Ranch in late autumn or early winter — for some reason the service apparently didn't think it would occur to the bison to move downhill to milder climes on their own as wintry conditions dictated. At the ranch the herd could be more easily watched over during their vulnerable season and also concentrated for the purposes of winter feeding. The buffalo drive was done on horseback by rangers and "most anybody [else] that could ride a horse," and there was some small element of danger involved. By the time of year when the bison drive occurred temperatures could be subzero and the snow was often belly deep to the horses. In spite of specially designed, deeply cleated shoes, horses often slipped on ice and snow when pursuing the beasts, and participants in the drives would "once in a while...look back to see how many [of their fellows] had suffered spills or horses had fallen."

Fall roundups continued through 1938, and on at least one occasion rangers intentionally used the drive to haze a new recruit in their fraternity. It is a story indicative of different values in a different era, and involves a man named Bob LaCombe, who was chief buffalo keeper during the 1920s. All accounts of LaCombe recount his toughness, and indeed he was a military veteran of grim action in the Philippines in the late nineteenth century. He was also one of the original set of rangers hired when the National Park Service took control of Yellowstone in 1916. La-Combe's toughness and rugged background probably contributed to a rowdy sense of humor which, when combined with that rougher time and place in which they lived, led LaCombe and some other veteran rangers to maneuver a herd of buffalo into a corral at the Buffalo Ranch in such a way that a new enlistee named Ted Ogston was nearly run over in the stampede. Ted got out of the way by climbing to the top of a fence post, while the herders, which included Harry Trischman, "just about fell off their horses laughing." Ogston didn't share in their mirth, however, at least not at the time.

Once the bison herd was caught up and corralled at the Buffalo Ranch, the hard work of separating the animals for various procedures like inoculations and castrations began. Chutes to funnel and immobilize the animals were used, but still the work demanded a high degree of physical effort in wintry conditions. And beginning in the mid 1920s, rangers were called upon to cull the Yellowstone bison herd. This somewhat surprising turn of events, which came about just two decades after the Yellowstone population had bottomed out and there had been real and justifiable concern that the species would disappear from the park, was a result of the success of the Lamar ranching operation. Of course the success of the ranching operation was reflective of the ideology that had created it, and as such it was in a way deceiving. While the raw numbers of bison present could be seen as heartening — by 1924 the captive herd count was 753 — the herd was a product of manipulations such as veterinary care, supplemental feeding, and a selective breeding program orchestrated according to the standards and values of its human handlers. The resulting herd could not be considered truly wild, and among some park service circles it never was intended to be. Many in the

service, principally then superintendent Horace M. Albright, wanted the captive herd to serve as a readily visible roadside attraction for the visiting public. Albright hoped that the easily spotted animals would thrill park visitors and thus help build a constituency for the nascent National Park Service.

As early as 1910, just eight years after the captive herd had been started and when it totaled only 120 animals, the acting superintendent for some reason wanted to do away with some bulls. By 1915, when the ranched herd numbered 239, the then superintendent wanted to cull one hundred or more males. Throughout the ranching period, lone bull bison that refused to be driven or handled were dubbed "outlaws" — that is literally the word that was used. The choice of the word "outlaw" is interesting, especially remembering how the earlier scouts and army troopers had used the word "scalp" to refer to the cape or pelt of a bison's head and foreparts, or the portion of the animal used for mounting by a taxidermist. It was as though early park residents were trying to preserve something of the Old West with the use of selective terminology.

National Park Service

Roundup at the Buffalo Ranch attracted a crowd representing a cross-section of park society, as evidenced by this January 14, 1940 photograph. The frozen moment in time seems to capture the essence of such an operation, where individuals involved are nervously trying to figure out their roles while simultaneously jockeying for social standing within the hierarchy present at the scene. The tensions were leavened, of course, by the large imposing beasts and the impending deaths of many of those animals. Note the riders on horseback in the corral in the background.

Captured elk are transferred from a stock truck to an enclosed rail car at the railroad head in Gardiner, Montana. Vapor from the animals' panicked breathing can be seen rising from the back of the truck. For decades elk considered surplus in Yellowstone were shipped live to bolster depleted herds elsewhere.

Rangers often shot and killed outlaw bulls out on the range they steadfastly refused to leave.

If the service had a master plan in mind for all bison, and eliminated those bison that refused to comply with the plan, it also had a blueprint in mind for the range the animals inhabited. The rangers' take on the range mostly had to do with its perceived productivity and an estimation of how many animals it could support. Much of the thinking of the day was derived from the paradigms of contemporary livestock production, and withal appraisals of the range and its potential productivity in terms of wildlife populations varied considerably through time. Not surprisingly, park service managers often used mathematics to arrive at their population and range decisions, applying elaborate formulas with multipliers and divisors to justify actions they had already concluded to make for reasons which were as mysterious as a individual ranger wanting to shoot an outlaw bull buffalo grazing by himself out in the hills. The upshot of all this was a program that either culled the Yellowstone bison herd or allowed it to grow depending on the notions of park managers.

Most culling occurred in the winter, during Yellowstone's bottleneck season and also the season of the year when bison were collected and therefore accessible at the Buffalo Ranch. Early on, only bull bison

were culled, although there was a policy of eliminating "cripples" in the herd as well. Apparently bison had to pass standards of physical appearance as well as standards of behavior. Bison were not only killed on site, but also loaded on trucks for shipment to slaughterhouses. Rangers built a slaughterhouse of their own at the Buffalo Ranch in 1928, where they sometimes killed and butchered the animals themselves rather than shipping them off to slaughterhouses elsewhere. Some animals were also loaded for shipment to other reserves where they were used to start new herds or to supplement existing herds.

By 1934 park service officials were able to review the history of removals from the tame herd and note that by that year a total of 682 had been shipped to slaughterhouses, 48 outlaws and cripples had been destroyed in the park, and 297 had been shipped off for live stocking elsewhere. That year, 1934, was also the first year when live shipments were made to Indian tribes. Both the Crow and the Oglala Sioux received shipments that year, which they used as seed stock to begin their own herds. Other herds begun or supplemented with stock from Yellowstone include herds in the Henry Mountains of Utah, Grand Teton National Park, Fort Niobrara National Wildlife Refuge in Nebraska, Wind Cave National Park in South Dakota, and others.

Yellowstone officials realized that live shipments of bison to start new herds elsewhere would not keep the park population in line with their view of where it should be. As Chief Ranger Francis LaNoue noted, "It is unlikely that we will have many requests like that of the Crow Reservation where numbers taken are sufficient...." Other measures taken at least partly to hold down the size of the Lamar herd included trucking 71 of the animals to Hayden Valley and Fountain Flats to restock that part of the park. More than just reducing the size of the Lamar herd, however, or redistributing bison for ecological reasons, the restocking of the central range to form what eventually would be called

Photographs documenting elk herd reduction by
National Park Service personnel in the late 1940s
illustrate the assembly-line nature of their slaugh-
ter-to-processing work.

National Park Service Archives

National Park Service

Buffalo Bill Historical Center • Jack Richard

Penned elk make an easy target for reduction at the Slough Creek elk trap (above left). National Park Service employees work with a bull elk in the Crystal Creek elk trap, circa 1960s (top right). Elk were funneled by a helicopter into a holding corral (below) prior to working individual animals in chutes.

the Mary Mountain herd was done to improve bison viewing opportunities for park visitors.

After culling mostly bulls in the early days of bison management, rangers began killing or shipping cows and calves in considerable numbers in the winter of 1931-32. The roundup with horses ended in 1938, after which hay sprinkled on the snow was used to lure bison into corrals at the Buffalo Ranch. In later years helicopters were used in place of horses to do the shepherding, and failing with their driving attempts rangers sometimes resorted to shooting bison in the field. Winter herd reductions in Yellowstone continued until the winter of 1966-67, and on occasion whittled the park herd down to levels that seem very low by today's standards. At the end of the 1966 reductions, for example, the bison herd was left with a post reduction count of just 266, and there were other years prior to that when the census yielded just a few hundred animals. These numbers compare to counts in the 3500-5000 range in Yellowstone today. All through the period of bison ranching and herd reductions peculiar mental processes prevailed among park managers. In 1967, the management plan called for reducing the Pelican Valley segment of the herd

to 180 animals. When a pre-reduction survey found only 175 bison, rangers shot 34 anyway. And perhaps most fundamentally of all, the underlying lunacy of working with one hand to raise herd numbers through elimination of predators, supplemental feeding, and inoculation against disease, while simultaneously culling the herd to keep numbers down — well, that contradiction seems not to have occurred to anyone involved in the bloody affair. The program was akin to applying massive amounts of chemical fertilizer to a garden to enhance plant growth while simultaneously spraying the garden with herbicide to keep the plants in check.

During the same winters when rangers were employed with concurrently boosting and butchering the bison herd, they were also engaged in similar activities with Yellowstone's elk. Actually, because elk were (and still are) by far the most numerous large ungulate in Yellowstone, elk trapping and herd reductions were done on a much larger scale than similar operations with bison. Rather than just one capture facility, such as the corrals at the Buffalo Ranch for bison, a number of elk traps were constructed at different locations across the northern range.

Elk were never ranched intensively in the manner that bison were husbanded at the Buffalo Ranch, but at times they were supplementally fed during the winter months. The elk also benefited from predator control, particularly the efforts that eliminated the park's wolves and all but eliminated its mountain lions. There probably are no data to prove it, but elk populations may also have increased because of an absence of predation by bears. To a great extent Yellowstone's bears fed on garbage for most of the park's first century of existence and to some degree their attentions consequently were focused away from elk. Today both black and grizzly bears take a considerable number of elk calves in the spring and early summer when the calves are still small enough to be vulnerable. And grizzlies take some adults all through the

seasons that bears are out of their dens, especially in the autumn when they kill a disproportionate number of bulls while they are distracted by the rut and more easily stalked.

Elk were hit hard by market hunters in Yellowstone during the 1870s and early 1880s, and their numbers were greatly reduced by the hide hunting that mostly occurred on the park's Northern Range in the winter. Though much reduced in population, the park's elk were never seriously threatened with extinction in the way that bison were, and indeed elk populations rebounded quite quickly after hunting in Yellowstone was banned in 1883. By the winter of 1910-1911 there were enough elk on the Northern Range that large numbers of them were flushed out of the park by that year's wintry weather. As the elk migrated down the Yellowstone River corridor north of the park, which was the ancestral route their forebears had always followed to escape harsh conditions in Yellowstone's high country, they damaged farmers' fences and haystacks. In response to the problem of too many elk, 800 of the animals were shipped from the park, as Yellowstone commenced a program of live trapping elk for shipment elsewhere. Most elk were shipped to states from which elk had been extirpated, where they were used to establish replacement herds.

In the early days, rangers used hay to lure elk into the traps. When a sufficient number of elk had gathered inside the enclosures to feed on the scattered hay, rangers closed the gates and then began processing the animals through systems of funnels and chutes. As was done with bison, helicopters were used in later times to herd elk off the range and into corrals. Again as with bison, live trapping and shipment never could keep up with increases in herd numbers, so rangers began a program of shooting the elk out on the range.

Surplus World War II military vehicles known as the M29 Weasel became an effective tool for retrieving elk shot in the roadless backcountry. In the photo to the right, carcasses have been stockpiled at the road for pick up later on.

National Park Service

National Park Service

Shooting on the range increased after the advent of over snow vehicles capable of negotiating Yellowstone's snowy terrain. These tracked vehicles, some of which were known as "weasels," not only had the ability to move through snow, they also had enough power to drag multiple elk carcasses back to park roads, where they were loaded onto waiting trucks for shipment out of the park. Most of the elk meat resulting from herd reductions was given to regional Indian reservations.

Truly astonishing numbers of elk were removed from Yellowstone through the first seven decades of the 20th century. Combining live shipments, animals killed by rangers within the park, and animals killed outside the park by hunters in Montana (and this last category was almost always the smallest contribution within a given year's total), annual reductions of 2,000 to 4,000 elk were common. Sometimes the totals reached 6,000 to 7,000 in a single winter. Again as was the case with the park's bison, elk were at the mercy of park managers, and decisions as to whether allow the elk population to grow or be culled were based on varying interpretation of the condition of the Northern Range and how many ungulates it was thought the range could support. Yellowstone elk reductions came to an end in the winter of 1966-1967, when a comparatively low total of 1,100 elk were removed. Changing attitudes within the park service with regard to nature, as well as substantial outcry from various public constituencies brought elk reductions to an end late in that winter. Post reduction tallies that winter found only 3,172 elk left on the Northern Range, which was only a fraction of the totals that had been there in most winters earlier in the century. It is also interesting to note that only about thirty years later, in spite of mortality from winter weather, predators, human hunters

State and national tempers flared as the result of a massive Northern elk herd reduction during the winter of 1961-1962. Montana and Wyoming sportsmen associations sought federal restraining orders to halt National Park Service herd reductions and area newspapers, like the Park County [Montana] News (above) published special issues decrying the "slaughter." To draw national attention to the issue, a young Butte, Montana guide and outfitter hitchhiked to Washington D.C. carrying a mounted elk head and a petition which he hoped to present to President John F. Kennedy. The young outfitter later became known as Evel Knievel, America's iconic motorcycle daredevil. National Park Service elk reductions ended in 1967.

outside the park, and other factors, that core group of elk survivors had multiplied to a herd of nearly 20,000 animals. They are a fecund and resilient species.

During the winters that Yellowstone's rangers were intensively managing the park's elk and bison, they were also trapping and shooting the park's remnant herd of pronghorn antelope. Mostly done on winter range near the park's north boundary, this work was also intended to hold the pronghorn population in line with what the agency thought was the carrying capacity of the range. And the reduction efforts were made in spite of the fact that Yellowstone's pronghorn herd is isolated from other antelope, and may even be somewhat distinctive from other groups.

Predator control also took a lot of the rangers' time, at least until 1936. When considered from today's perspective, Yellowstone's predator elimination program in the early 20th century is nothing short of mind blowing. Between 1904 and 1935 park records show that 121 mountain lions were killed in the park. During the same time period, 132 wolves were eliminated, and coyotes suffered a whooping loss of 4,352 killed in action. These numbers obviously do not include predators killed before 1904, of which there were many.

Predators were killed not just by shooting, but also by trapping and poisoning. Trapping and poisoning are indiscriminate, and unquestionably both methods led to a lot of collateral damage in untargeted species. As scavengers, wolverines and skunks seemed especially to have suffered serious losses from feeding on carcasses laced with poison. From early records in the park, it seems that wolverines were quite common. Skunks were, too, at least in the lower elevations of the park around Mammoth. Nowadays neither species is seen in Yellowstone with any frequency, and suppositiously it seems reasonable to think the neither species was able to recover from the anti-predator blitz. Other species killed by poison included eagles, ravens, magpies, foxes, pine martens, and probably others. Even the tallies of targeted species are cast into doubt when considering how many animals must have moved some distance away from poisoning stations before expiring, and therefore were not included in body counts. This doubt would be in addition to the skepticism inherent with dealing with statistics accumulated by any bureaucracy, if for no other reason than the fact that bureaucratic personnel tend to be discontinuous. But even if the Park Service statistics are taken at face value, a lot of predators died. Wolves and mountain lions were eliminated completely from Yellowstone, although lions managed to repopulate the park on their own a few years after the predator control program ceased. Wolves, on the other hand, did not return in viable numbers until the official re-introduction efforts of 1995 and 1996, which brought in replacement wolves from Alberta and British Columbia.

By the nature of climate in Yellowstone, most predator control work took place during the winter, when the animals tended to be more visible and vulnerable. The rangers' annual cycle also lent itself to doing the predator control work in winter. Rangers were tied up with matters involving park visitors in the summer, whereas they had more free time in the winter, especially during those days in the early 20th century when winter visitation was virtually nonexistent.

————

A pair of mountain lion hunters (left) posing with a lion killed somewhere on the range in Yellowstone during predator control efforts in 1927 contrasts remarkably with a 1930 photograph of Superintendent Roger Toll and many others "oohing and aahing" over a pet mountain lion at Mammoth.

90   WINTER HOTEL CONSTRUCTION

Winter Hotel Construction

"To Build in a Winter Wilderness the Grand Chateau"

Snow squalls and sunset over the Old Faithful Inn, February 1997.

Through Yellowstone National Park's history there have been a number of large construction projects conducted during the winter season. Reasons for working on projects necessarily exposed to the elements during the park's notoriously cold and snowy winter include a desire to avoid summer crowds, and in some cases to take advantage of a seasonally underemployed work force. The primary reasons for working in the winter, however, have always been financial. Like the mad dogs and Englishmen of the era who were foolish enough to venture into the midday sun of their tropical colonies, Yellowstone's businessmen were more than willing to expose their workers to the blast of midwinter blizzards in the interest of financial considerations.

Two winter construction projects in particular stand out in the park's winter history, first because of the epic nature of the projects themselves and second because of the grandiosity of the results of those projects. The two were the construction of the Old Faithful Inn during the winter of 1903-1904, and the building of the Canyon Hotel during the winter of 1910-1911. Both projects were the creations of an outstanding young architect named Robert C. Reamer. The projects were orchestrated and financed by Harry

Child and his Yellowstone Park Association as well as by YPA's parent company, the Northern Pacific Railroad.

The first of these building projects, the Old Faithful Inn, is the only one of the two structures still in existence. Contrary to much popular belief, the Inn was not entirely built in the winter. In fact, construction commenced on or about June 12, 1903, and the shell of the building was largely complete by the onset of true winter later that year. The exterior frame of the building may have been "dried in," but workmen still had much finish work to do in the chilled and gloomy interior of the structure. They had to have been a tough bunch, those workmen. There is sufficient evidence to believe that the Inn's massive chimney and its eight fireplaces (four small, four very large) were finished and operational by the beginning of winter, so they would have supplied some degree of heating in that central portion of the building. But the fireplaces would have done nothing to heat the wings of the original Old House, and even in the lobby around the chimney the space is so cavernous and the structure so completely uninsulated that any amount of heat dissipated almost immediately through windows and walls, and especially through the Inn's vast ceiling.

There were no portable propane heaters to warm immediate work areas, as there are today. Electricity, if present at all, would have been minimal, probably

Facing page, Yellowstone's most well known building in winter raiment, 1982.

just enough for a few lights in common areas and certainly not enough for any supplemental heat, or for any electrically powered tools even if they had existed. (The first electrically powered circular saw, for example, wasn't patented until 1923.) No, it was hand tools manipulated in ambient natural light coming through the windows, with the work done in conditions varying from just plain cold to downright frigid. This issue of lighting seems especially significant — the Old Faithful Inn crew accomplished an amazing amount of work during the winter of 1903-1904, even given the fact that the shell of the building was almost certainly completed before the beginning of winter. To have accomplished what they did using only available natural light makes their accomplishments all the more impressive, as their work days were limited to the brief period of daylight during short winter days. And even if the workmen tried to extend their working hours by using lantern or candle light, the light from such sources is dim. It would have been mighty tough to see things like subtle pencil lines marking the spot where a piece of wood needed to be cut. However the craftsmen overcame the challenges to their working conditions, the fact that they did so is illustrated by the artistry and magnitude of their work, which fortunately still exists for all of us to admire today.

Where the workmen stayed during the winter construction period is another mystery. Logic would strongly suggest that the crew had heated sleeping quarters somewhere. Quality rest in quarters that were at least tepid would have been a necessity after so much hard work in freezing and otherwise difficult conditions. But where that might have been is unknown. The lobby had some little bit of heat, as has been discussed, but it doesn't seem logical that the men would have bunked there. For one thing, it wouldn't have been warm, no matter how much firewood they stoked into the fireplaces. For another reason, the lobby would logically have been the focal point for construction work, and so would have been cluttered with tools and materials, as well as covered with sawdust and dirt — which would not have presented a very comforting or restful space, and sleeping there involved laying out bedding materials every evening and then rolling them back up every morning so they could be stashed somewhere out the way.

Tents had been used during winter in the Old Faithful area for at least 15 years before the construction of the Inn, so perhaps they were employed to house the crew, or perhaps one was used as a mess hall. But tents present their own challenges in such a cold and snowy climate. They are prone to collapse under snow loads,

A stereoscopic view of the Old Faithful Inn under construction in the autumn of 1903, illustrates that construction of the building was well along before real winter set in. The Inn opened for its first season on June 1, 1904.

and snow cleared from the roofs of tents would have piled up against the walls and pressed inward on the flimsy fabric. And at Old Faithful the cold and snowy nature of the climate was exacerbated by the large amount of vapor that percolates from so much of the ground in the area, moisture that would immediately condense and then crystallize into frost when contacting the inside of cold tent canvas. Another possibility is that some portion of the Inn itself was temporarily adapted to serve as mess facility and heated sleeping quarters. Still another possibility is that some temporary structure was erected nearby to serve rooming and boarding functions, but again it simply isn't known. In the absence of firm evidence any conclusion about such matters is at best an educated guess.

A huge challenge for the Inn's construction workers would have been dealing with accumulations of snow. The roof and walls of the building were intact before winter set in, yes, but snow piling up on the roof presented a problem that had to be removed. Worse still, there probably was some low level of heat in the building, from the lobby's fireplace if nothing else. It takes only a small amount of heat inside a structure to melt snow on its roof, and the resulting melt water naturally flows downward, past the exterior walls of the building, and then refreezes into ice dams on the exposed eaves. These ice dams on the eaves grow progressively, and subsequent melt water backs up behind the barriers and then leaks into the inside of the building. The ice dams have to be broken so that new melt water coming down the roof has somewhere to drain, and ideally snow above the occupied portion of the building is shoveled off before it has a chance to melt and to feed the cycle. For the construction workers on the Inn, this would have amounted to a lot of ice smashing and snow shoveling over a lot of square feet of roof expanse.

More shoveling would have been required on the ground, too, where a laborer had to struggle against gravity rather than using it to his advantage, as he was able to do when shoveling snow off a roof. Snow would have accumulated against the walls of the structure, where in some places it would have been in the way of necessary tasks, and it also accumulated in doorways and against windows. Doors had to be kept open for obvious reasons, and windows had to be kept clear so that they could admit the light essential for interior work. And without question most building materials had to be stacked in the open, somewhere outside the building, where they were buried by each snowfall and had to be shoveled off whenever the materials were needed for the work in progress.

The hardy construction crew of the Old Faithful Inn, posed on a snowbank in front of the building in the spring of 1904.

The construction crew did have one big advantage in that it appears that a considerable volume of construction materials had been accumulated on site at Old Faithful prior to the building of the Inn. The powers present, chiefly Harry Child, had desired to replace existing hostelries in the Old Faithful area for some time before 1903. While the evolution of what that replacement ultimately would be was still progressing, an evolution that of course would lead to Robert Reamer's famous design for the Old Faithful Inn, Harry Child was moving in the direction of preparing to build *something* in the area. Toward that end, Child arranged to station one hundred horses at Old Faithful during the winter of 1902-1903, the winter previous to the commencement of work on the Inn. The plan was to use those draft animals to haul construction materials from the railhead in Gardiner and to stockpile them in the Upper Geyser Basin. Child also must have assigned a fair number of men to Old Faithful to manage the stock, and to drive the eighteen four horse teams that were used to do the freighting. There must have been some sort of winter-worthy accommodations for both men and horses there as early as that winter.

Apparently Harry Child thought that continuous travel by the four horse teams would keep the park's roads open for wagons through the winter. But unless the snow that winter was exceptionally light, the wagons must have been converted to or replaced by sleighs at some point, although that is not recorded. A newspaper in Livingston, Montana did report in late January, however, that "the work of transporting the lumber to the upper geyser basin [sic] for the hotel

Teamsters hauling freight to the Canyon Hotel during the winter of 1910-1911 take a break on the Canyon-Norris road. This image was made in late winter or early spring.

on either snowshoes or cross country skis as he reconnoitered through the forest. Mr. Sargent reported that it was surprisingly difficult to find the 3,000 suitable trees he had been assigned to locate. This really does seem surprising, given the facts that lodgepoles are so common in Yellowstone and that Sargent was on his reconnaissance in the days before much logging for in-park construction projects had taken place, as well as prior to the forest fires which have become so prevalent in more recent times. Interestingly, even in late January of 1903, the newspaper account about James Sargent related that he was looking for logs to be used in the construction, "...of the new log cottages at the Upper basin [sic]. In building the eight or ten buildings about 3,000 logs will be required...." So at that time it was not clearly understood that this older plan for building a number of smaller "cottages" in the Upper Geyser Basin was to be replaced with plans to build the Old Faithful Inn. Nevertheless, the effort to build the latter structure unquestionably benefited from the preliminary work done by people like James Sargent, as well as from the efforts of the teamsters who had amassed so much building material at the site before the beginning of construction work in June of 1904.

The next winter, when construction on the Old Faithful Inn was going full-bore, the teamsters involved with hauling the massive amounts of additional material needed for the ongoing project must also have benefited from the experiences of the freighting operation of the winter before. Those teamsters, if anything, had it tougher than the construction workers laboring on the building itself. The freighters were obviously exposed to the open elements for the entire duration of each trip, and they had to battle the elements beyond what it took to simply stay alive out there. They had to handle teams that were fractious at times, for the animals themselves were being forced to toil in an environment which was decidedly unnatural for horses. Both teamsters and horses had to fight their way through massive drifts in wind-protected spots, and through Yellowstone famously deep and fluffy snow pretty much everywhere else. They also had to negotiate many up and down grades on the road from Gardiner to Old Faithful. Upgrades must

there is progressing rapidly," so whether by wagon or by sleigh the teams and the teamsters were able to successfully transport the construction materials through the course of the winter.

Another newspaper account, this one from a publication in Gardiner, reported that a man named James Sargent had been engaged during the winter in the Old Faithful area for the purpose of searching out suitable stands of lodgepole pines as a source of logs for the building project, a duty he must have performed

National Park Service

Freighters (above) and sleds loaded with construction material bound for Canyon pause near Willow Park. At right, a teamster negotiates the narrow ascent at the Golden Gate where the road from Mammoth Hot Springs pops out onto Swan Lake Flat. Records indicate that teamsters used two-handed snow shovels to scoop chunks of snow out of the massive drift ahead of the horses. The teamster then dumped the snow over the edge of the road into the Glen Creek chasm. It is highly likely that the teamsters learned the snow removal technique from park winterkeepers, and patterned their two-handed shovels after models already in use by roof shovelers in the park.

have been taxing pulls with questionable footing for the teams, of course. And depending on snow and road conditions, downgrades could have been treacherous, too, for how do you brake a sleigh?

Special "snow" shoes were no doubt fitted to the draft horses to provide extra traction on snow and ice. These shoes have cleats up to 3/8" or so in length that bite into snow and ice in the way a football player's cleats bite into sod, and these cleated shoes certainly would have been a benefit going either uphill or down. The problem of downhill runaways would have been greater in late winter and spring, when the packed roads melted a bit on the surface during a period of warm sunshine, and then refroze when the cold came on again. There is at least one photo taken during the construction of the Canyon Hotel in 1911 of freighters and their sleighs on the Canyon-Norris road that shows the road surface in just such a glazed condition. The roads likely went through the same springtime pattern of melting and refreezing during construction of the Old Faithful Inn in 1904.

But, because of the freighting operation the winter before, at least there must have been bunks for the men and barns for the horses at Old Faithful. And the sleigh drivers, who presumably included many of the same men in both winters, must have picked up a few

tricks on how to accomplish the job during that first winter of operation. It was still rough duty, however, as indicated by the records of a similar freighting operation a few years later. This account is from the experiences of teamsters hired to transport material for the building of the Canyon Hotel during the winter of 1910-1911, and describes some of the problems encountered on the wintry trail: *"Horses downed in the drifts, loads overturned, sleds broken, harness torn apart, snow slides and sudden blizzards increased the hardships, the hindrances and the perils of the gigantic task....In our...journey through this strange and rigorous scene, we passed snow-covered piles of freight that had been set beside the trail from overloaded sleighs, waiting to be hauled almost piecemeal over miles of nearly insurmountable difficulty."* Things couldn't have been much different for the freighters engaged in hauling freight to the Old Faithful Inn.

Even though large stores of lumber and other materials had been stockpiled beforehand at Old Faithful, there still was a lot more to be hauled during the winter of the Inn's construction. Gardiner newspaper accounts note how the boiler for the Inn, which must have been a massive unit and therefore probably required special measures on the part of the men and teams assigned to transport it, passed through that town en route to the Upper Geyser Basin. Other reports describe the shipment of a mind boggling 800,000 pounds of nails for the endeavor. Again to use records from the Canyon Hotel project as a yardstick, a typical payload on a horse drawn sleigh in these wintry conditions was about 2,500 pounds, which translated to a total of about 50 sleigh loads to transport the freight from one railroad car.

The roads apparently held up for much of the winter while the Inn was being constructed, or perhaps more accurately they were kept open by the passage of so much traffic, for there are a number of newspaper accounts of construction contractors coming and going through the course of the winter between the Upper Geyser Basin and the towns of Gardiner

Draft horses lean into their sled harness against the strain of an 8,000 pound payload — the electric generator bound for Canyon Hotel.

and Livingston, Montana. Yellowstone dignitaries, including the park superintendent John Pitcher, as well as Harry Child himself, also were able to come and go on official inspections. But deterioration of the roads was inevitable as the season progressed and the snow deepened. This seems to be indicated by an account of Harry Child's experience when he returned for another visit in March of 1904, this time accompanied by his wife Adelaide. Harry and Adelaide made it to Old Faithful apparently without excessive challenge, but a heavy snowstorm while they were on location stranded them for several days. A reasonable assumption is that after that period of a few days the new snow had set up to some extent and thereby made the roads more negotiable. A further and equally reasonable assumption would be that some of the teamsters on Child's payroll, undoubtedly tougher and more skilled than either Mr. or Mrs. Child, pioneered the

route ahead of the couple's departure and broke the trail for them.

The biggest mystery surrounding the construction of the Old Faithful Inn is that it *is* such a mystery. The project was the biggest thing going in the park at the time, by far the biggest thing going, and yet there is very little information recorded about the yearlong construction phase of the building, or even about its initial opening on June 1, 1904. It has been suggested that attention at the time of the Inn's construction and opening was distracted by newsworthy events which were occurring elsewhere in the world. Chief among these suggested distractions was the 1904 World's Fair in St. Louis, organized in part to commemorate the 100th anniversary of the Louisiana Purchase, although for that commemoration it was a year late.

Yes, the World's Fair was going on, and unquestionably it was a big deal. And the Wright Brothers were contemporaneous with the construction of the Inn when they flew at Kitty Hawk on December 17, 1903, and there were definitely other items in the news at the time. But there is always something going on elsewhere in the world, and it is also true that to a great extent Yellowstone was and still is a realm unto itself. This latter phenomenon must have been even more pronounced in 1903 and 1904, in the days before computers, television and even AM radio, than it is today.

So it is a profound mystery why records about the Inn's construction are so sparse. As far as it is known, there are no journals from any of the workmen who built the Inn. Robert Reamer the architect had no diary, nor did Harry Child the capitalist. Logbook entries about the project from soldier stations in the park are either curt or mum. There are only two known photographs of the building under construction, as well as one more of the construction crew assembled on a snowbank in front of the building in what is obviously a late winter or more likely an early spring portrait, or in other words when the construction was nearly complete. A primary question that arises here is where was F. Jay Haynes, the famous photographer who beginning in 1881 devoted so much of his life to photographing all things Yellowstone? It seems like Haynes would have jumped on the Old Faithful Inn project with both feet, and would have been eager to document the project from beginning to end. But no Haynes photos of the Inn appear until the summer of 1904, after the building had already opened for its first tourist season.

There is always the possibility, of course, that long forgotten records about the Old Faithful Inn's construction will resurface. Perhaps someone will find a stash from a grandfather or a great uncle in an attic somewhere, and the stash will contain a journal that the old relative kept while he was working on the building of the Inn, or while he was driving one of those four horse teams over snowbound park roads to haul materials for the construction. Alternately, someone may discover a long lost assortment of photographs taken during the construction of Yellowstone's most famous structure. But well over 100 years have passed since the original Old House of the Old Faithful Inn was constructed, and no treasure trove of information about its construction has surfaced so far. Realistically, the chance of a significant new discovery of such material grows less and less with each passing year.

Fortunately there is a fair amount of surviving information about the construction of the Canyon Hotel — a lot more than what there is about the construction of the Old Faithful Inn. Much like the Inn, construction of the Canyon Hotel began in the summer, and the frame and the exterior of the structure were mostly complete by the onset of winter. Then work continued through the following winter, that of 1910-1911, to complete the inside of the building. The great tragedy of the Canyon Hotel is that it was a magnificent creation that sadly no longer exists. In fact, the huge hotel, which still has the distinction of having been the largest building ever to

exist in Yellowstone, was fated to serve only through the 1958 summer season. After that, for reasons that smacked of a combination of shady politics, financial manipulations, and problems with the unstable ground on which the hotel had been sited, the building was condemned, stripped of salvageable scrap, and then burned in 1960.

Much of what is known about this construction project was recorded in a neat little booklet titled "A Miracle in Hotel Building," with a subtitle that reads "The Dramatic Story of the Building of the New Canyon Hotel in Yellowstone Park." It was written by a man named John H. Raftery, who was the editor of a newspaper in Butte, Montana. It appears that the fact finding trip Raftery made to Canyon in January of 1911 in preparation for writing his booklet had been arranged by Harry Child of the Yellowstone Park Hotel Company. At least Child and his company later published Raftery's resulting pamphlet, and a strong suspicion is that by facilitating Raftery's journalism, Child was trying to avoid a repeat of his regrettable oversight in not publicizing either the construction or the opening of the Old Faithful Inn seven years earlier.

Raftery, who often used the initials J.H. in his byline, made the trip from Gardiner to Canyon in one of the horse-drawn sleighs used to haul construction ma-

Architect Robert Reamer (left) and construction foreman Mr. H.L. George take a break on a pile of materials in front of the Canyon Hotel. The date of this photograph was October 1910, and shows that the project was well advanced before the onset of winter.

terials to the job site. Presumably, he rode in a sleigh that was loaded with more than just the journalist and his note tablet, and he described his trip thusly:

"Through a blinding blizzard, with the wind blowing a horizontal gale of thirty miles an hour, over thirty-seven miles of almost trackless snow, four feet on the level, through mountain gorges, where the drift lay packed from ten to twenty feet, across frozen creeks and rivers, I had come in a horse-drawn sleigh to the brink of the Grand Canyon of the Yellowstone River in the National Park to witness the titanic winter work of building a new half-million dollar hotel that is to be ready for the summer visitor by June."

Elaborating on details of the trip, Raftery went on: *"In exposed reaches [wind-scoured sites that had blown free of snow] the runners ground and squeaked over the bare sand and rocks; in the protected defiles the surface of the thoroughfare was obliterated, lost in piles of flour-dry snow, heaped high against the side wall of the canyons and sloping away in perilous descent to the bottom of the gorges. Here the big scoop shovels came in play to open a passage for the team and sleigh until at length the road descended into the desolate Swan Lake flat, where the gale swept in unbridled fury across an arctic waste of undulous snow from four to ten feet deep.*

"For over three miles across the Swan Lake flat the road had long since been buried, and now the course of it, winding and uncertain, is marked at either side by little pine trees stuck into the snow by the freighters to mark the edge of the obliterated road. A misstep to either side plunges the horses floundering into from four to a dozen feet of snow, for the only footing is the six-inch snow pack made by the runners of the freight laden sleds creeping slowly over it in their long and perilous journey from the railroad station at Gardiner to the site of the new Canyon Hotel by the brink of the famous cataract of the Yellowstone.

"Low pitched, six horse, cumbrous sled-wagons, manned by stalwart, brave and skillful freighters, grind and crawl over the almost incredible difficulties of this arctic trail. All this winter they have been hauling lumber, hardware, cement, tiling, doors, windows, bath tubs, tools, machinery, supplies for men and horses. Ten million pounds in all they have hauled through boreal storms, over snow-jammed passes, across ice-bound rivers, along the dizzy brinks of narrow cliff trails, and with the thermometer seldom above zero and ranging down to forty degrees below."

Grandiloquent passage, perhaps, but most of it rings true and it is fortunate that Raftery completed this work, and equally fortunate that it has survived

The Canyon Hotel in winter. The building was and remains the largest structure ever built in Yellowstone National Park.

to the present. In all it is a good description of the freighting operation over the snow to Canyon, and without Raftery's account we obviously wouldn't know as much as we do. Elsewhere in his booklet, the newspaperman demonstrates that he was not willing to let literal interpretation of the facts stand in the way of dramatic presentation of the story, such as when he writes of a "slinking coyote, bold in starvation and gaunt as a skeleton, heading for the settlement to steal a meal or find a grave." In all of Yellowstone's history it is doubtful if any coyote has ever robbed a grave, at least not since the time of the Indians and the mountain men, but again, we are lucky to have what Raftery left us. And it probably was true that Harry Child had recruited him to be a booster, so that was his role.

Raftery could hear construction work in progress even before he arrived at the Canyon Hotel site, the sound of which he described as "volleys of clattering hammers." In another bit of dramatic exaggeration, he related how cooks on the newly installed stoves heated gallons upon gallons of nails to serve to the carpenters at work, with the implication that heated nails would be kinder to hands and fingers. Logic would suggest, however, that heated nails would progress in short order from the point where they were too hot to handle to as cold as they would have been in the first place. That would be true even for large nails, for even the largest spikes don't really have that much mass and wouldn't retain heat for very long, so it doesn't seem like either the cooks or the carpenters would have invested much time in that program. The interior of the hotel-under-construction at best would have been very chilly, so by the time nails could have been carried from the kitchen to where they were needed they would have been cold again. And the cooks probably had plenty enough work to do without having to tie up their ranges by cooking nails.

If Raftery's figures are correct, that 10,000,000 pounds of freight were hauled in by sleigh, and that the average load was 2,500 pounds, then simple arithmetic yields a total of 4,000 sleigh loads for that winter. Throw in the assumption that transporting by sleigh began in mid-November and carried on through mid-May, and a total of 180 days of hauling is derived. Using that 180 day figure and little more arithmetic yields an average of 20-25 loads per day for the winter hauling season. Given the fact that the

Architect Robert Reamer (foreground) joins a celebratory baseball game on skis played by the construction crew of the Canyon Hotel in late winter/early spring 1911.

frame and exterior of the Canyon Hotel were complete by the time the first permanent snows fell in November, it seems safe to assume that the bulk of the construction materials had hauled by wagon during the summer and autumn of 1910. And it is recorded that there was at least one saw mill in the Canyon area in the years before the construction of the Canyon Hotel. Perhaps the project benefited from lumber that had been stockpiled in the area, or at least was milled locally during the construction phase and so didn't have to be hauled a long distance.

There is another interesting point about the Canyon Hotel. The most memorable Canyon Hotel, the only one about which there is much awareness today, was actually the third hotel to be constructed in the area. The first hotel was built in 1886, and it provided important winter housing for some of the early travelers in wintry Yellowstone who were featured in earlier pages of this book. The first hotel at Canyon was a prefabricated structure which was never intended to have much longevity, and it served only through the 1889 season. The second hotel at Canyon was built in 1891, and the interesting tidbit is that the Canyon Hotel of 1911 simply encompassed the second hotel into its design. The second hotel remained a part of the third until the whole composite burned down in August of 1960.

A bit more is known about the life of the crew during the construction of the Canyon Hotel than is known about the workers who built the Old Faithful Inn. Again, to draw on J.H. Raftery: *"The two regi-*

ments of men who spent the winter of 1910-11 building this marvelous mountain hotel have been practically isolated from the world for months. They have worked always seven days of the week; they had no saloon or club or theater to beguile their time or bemuse their faculties, and even for the younger, pleasure-seeking workers there was no diversion, except the fierce thrill of gliding and coasting on skis over the glacier-like slopes of the desolate amphitheater which surrounded them. There is probably no other like example of hotel building in history, and the structure which is the result, the scene which it civilizes without desecrating, the strange region which it adorns without vulgarizing are all in keeping and in singular symmetry."

Raftery goes on to extol the amenities offered in the new hotel, claiming that they met or exceeded anything offered in Europe. He also played on the idea of how architect Robert Reamer managed to site and design the Canyon Hotel in a way that did not detract from its natural setting, including Reamer's well known quote, "I built it in keeping with the place where it stands. Nobody could improve upon that. To be at discord with the landscape would be almost a crime. To try to improve upon it would be an impertinence."

Noteworthy is the mention of how workers amused themselves by using skis in their leisure time. Some photos exist of the workers playing baseball on their skis later in the winter. Judging by the quality of the light in the photos and by the nature of the snowpack, it is apparent that the baseball game took place late in the winter, when construction work was presumably nearing an end, so maybe the game was something of an end-of-project celebration. Architect Reamer is also pictured as a player in the baseball game.

The Canyon Hotel was truly remarkable for both its size and its opulence. The Mission 66 development that replaced it was designed in a 1950s modernistic style that was almost universally deplored, both at the time it was built as well as ever since. Moreover, construction of the new Canyon Village was shoddy and the complex was built on ground that was at least as unstable, if not more so, than the site of the grand Canyon Hotel. It is unquestionably one of the great tragedies of Yellowstone's history that circumstances combined to deny its survival until the present time. The park and all of us are much poorer for its loss.

© Jeff Henry

The venerable Old Faithful Inn dressed in snowdrifts on a lovely evening in late winter 1986.

Clearing snow from roof of Hamilton Store at Canyon, 1999

Winterkeeping in Yellowstone

"There Is a Great Deal of Work to That, As Well As an Art"

Canyon Hamilton Store, February 1996

The term *Winterkeeper* is nearly unique to Yellowstone and has been used to refer to the hardy souls who have served as winter caretakers for the park's famous hotels and other structures since the late 1800s, or in other words since the park's earliest days as a designated reserve. From the beginning, winterkeepers were responsible for looking after park buildings to prevent theft and vandalism, and also to clear snow from roofs to protect them from Yellowstone's crushing snow loads. Readers of this book will recall that winterkeepers were present and offered invaluable assistance to many of Yellowstone's early day winter travelers and explorers.

It appears that a few people wintered at Mammoth Hot Springs during the 1870s, where they performed the function of looking after properties belonging to the government and to private concessionaires. But Mammoth's lower elevation and relatively mild climate made roof shoveling unnecessary most winters, and that fact coupled with a growing year round presence of administrative and protective personnel at park headquarters soon rendered Mammoth winterkeepers a thing of the past.

According to the great Yellowstone historian Aubrey Haines, the first caretaker to winter in the park's higher, snowier regions was George Marshall, who spent the winter of 1880-1881 with his wife Sarah and their four children at the Marshall Hotel at the mouth of Nez Percé Creek in the Lower Geyser Basin. The Marshalls' experience was somewhat atypical, in that they were looking after their own hotel; as the winterkeeping tradition evolved, most winterkeepers were employees hired by park concessions companies. The Marshalls were typical, however, in their zest for the winterkeeping life. Although they had been cautioned about the supposed health hazards associated with living in proximity to the vast volumes of steam issuing from geothermal outlets in their neighborhood, a phenomenon naturally accentuated by the cold air of winter, George Marshall related in a midwinter letter that "...we have thus far found it not only a delightful experience, but have found it the healthiest climate we have ever lived in. We have four small children (who won't stay indoors), and several men wintering with us. None of us have [sic] even caught a cold, [and] all are enjoying tip-top health...." Down through the decades, nearly all who have spent time winterkeeping in Yellowstone recall it as one of the happiest and most memorable experiences of their lives.

As the 1880s progressed the number of park winterkeepers increased to keep pace with the increase in new park properties. By 1887 there were winter caretakers stationed at the Lower Geyser Basin, Old Faithful, Canyon and Norris. It's hard for us living today to appreciate the solitude enjoyed by those people, or the degree of self-reliance that by neces-

An unidentified man examines a snow cornice at Bridge Bay Marina in March 1969. Note the layered lines in the cornice. Each layer represents a wind event, and each layered deposit extends beyond the margins of the one before, so that the cornice grows ever larger and outward as the winter progresses.

sity they had to achieve. Many winterkeepers became experts in mastering the skills required to function in the world of snow and cold where they lived, a tradition that continues with a few individuals still working winters in the park today. Yellowstone's history is full of stories of winterkeepers out-performing more officially sanctioned members of park society. It may be remembered, for example, how the members of the Schwatka Expedition floundered on their first official winter exploration of Yellowstone in 1887, and how on several different occasions the members of that party received succor from winterkeepers already on station in the park. On some occasions the help given by winterkeepers to the Schwatka party may even have been life-saving. Of course the irony was glaring. The lauded Schwatka party, which had been ballyhooed in the national press as brave and heroic for daring to enter snowbound Yellowstone, was nearly overcome by wintry conditions in the park, while at the same time winterkeepers and their families, including small children, were thriving in the same environment.

By mid to late December of most years, a winterkeeper's principal duty was and still is to shovel snow from the roofs of buildings in his charge. Because of Yellowstone's high elevation and other factors, the park receives impressive amounts of snowfall. Winters were almost certainly heavier in the park's early days than they are today, but even today snow accumulations on the roofs of buildings can be truly awesome. Several factors come into play, including a structure's architecture, its compass orientation, and its exposure to the wind, but packed snow on roofs can reach depths of 15 feet or more. Wind is possibly the most important of these factors, as prevailing southwesters invariably move a large portion of a building's snow load to north-facing and east-facing pitches where, shaded from the sun and insulated from the earth's heat by the dead air space in the vacant building below, it forms an incredibly hard and dense pack. Structures with valley or dormer complexes on leeward exposures collect especially impressive masses of snow, as well as even more impressive overhanging cornices on their eaves. Each successive windstorm adds a new layer of snow to the roof, and each layer rolls outward and extends the cornice a bit further out over nothingness, so not only does the dead weight of the snow on a roof increase as the winter progresses, the overhanging cornice also exerts greater and greater leverage on the eaves of the building. The leveraging effect of a snow cornice on a building's overhang could be compared to that experienced by a human being holding a heavy weight at the end of an outstretched arm.

Windblown snow packs more densely than snow that has not been blown before the wind, so drifted snow on leeward roof exposures is heavier for a given depth. And all snow settles as time goes by. Snowpack on a roof settles just from the force of gravity, and becomes even more dense for that reason as well. Historically, temperatures in Yellowstone rarely rose above freezing during the winter months, a phenomenon mostly still true today, so snow loads on roof structures simply become heavier and heavier through the course of the many months of winter. Snow loads of 150 pounds per square foot of roof surface, or even greater, occur during heavy winters. To ponder that much weight for a moment, a snow load of 150 pounds

per square foot translates to a total of 4,800 pounds that has to be supported by just one sheet of plywood on the decking of a roof. As a consequence, there are many instances in Yellowstone's history of buildings suffering structural damage or collapsing altogether under such enormous weights. The risk of allowing such tremendous loads of snow to remain on buildings is even more substantial in view of how frequently Yellowstone experiences seismic tremors. This last consideration is especially important when one recalls the point of how buildings are differentially loaded with snow that has been blown off windward roof exposures and has been deposited on leeward facets.

Another consequence of these tremendous amounts of snow that had to be removed from roofs was that Yellowstone's winterkeepers came up with some very clever techniques to do the job. For one example, on a roof that is sufficiently steep, a wire can be slipped between the snow pack and the shingles to cut the snow loose and precipitate an avalanche, sometimes with all the snow on the building sliding off at once. On roofs with lesser pitch, the snow pack can be sawed into refrigerator-sized blocks with an old fashioned

National Park Service

Longtime Yellowstone employees Herb Vaughn (left) and Mark "Doc" Watson struggle with a heavy block of snow at Canyon in 1995. The two men have somewhere around 30 years of roof shoveling experience between them, and the densely packed block of snow they were moving likely weighed close to 1000 pounds.

crosscut saw, after which the blocks can be skidded off the roof by balancing them on a square shovel blade. On flat roofs (it's hard to believe that anyone ever designed a flat roof for construction in Yellowstone, but there have been and are many of them) the snow can be sawed into blocks and then skidded off with a two-handed scoop shovel, which works a lot like a drag pan pulled behind a mule on earth moving projects in pre-bulldozer days. Presumably these techniques were developed fairly early on — consider how daunting it must have been to tackle a roof straining under the weight of several million pounds of snow with a shovel only. The innovation of the crosscut saw must have happened almost immediately, as original winterkeepers relied on huge amounts of firewood for heat and for cooking fuel, a reliance that continued well into the 20th Century. Cutting firewood in those days involved the use of crosscut saws, and the innovative, self-reliant people engaged in the winterkeeping business probably were quick to recognize the possibilities of using a saw to cut dense snow on rooftops into manageable cubes.

So far these time-tested techniques for removing snow from rooftops have resisted replacement by mechanized or motorized means. Snow throwers small enough to be manipulated on a slippery roof are simply overwhelmed by the mass and density of the snow pack, and cannot match the volume of snow that can be moved by a skilled winterkeeper using the old hand tools. Heavier equipment would be difficult or impossible to maneuver and would carry the risk of damaging a roof during its operation. This seems appropriate — there are enough machines in this world, and there is still a great deal of romance involved in the removal of such large amounts of snow with simple tools and human muscle power. As a 1923 observer wrote after observing a winterkeeper at work on the Old Faithful Inn, "There is a great deal of work to that, as well as an art."

Considering the risk that would seem to be inherent in roof-clearing work, there have been surprisingly few job-related injuries to winterkeepers through the years. In fact, park archives reveal only one. Howard O'Connor, a winterkeeper at Old Faithful, slid off the roof of the Old Faithful Inn in April of 1912 and fractured his lower leg. Some cavalry troopers of the United States Army who were stationed at Old Faithful at the time were able to set O'Connor's leg, which they did with the help of instructions relayed over the telephone from a doctor at Mammoth. Doing so, however, caused the fallen winterkeeper so much pain that he accused his rescuers of trying to murder

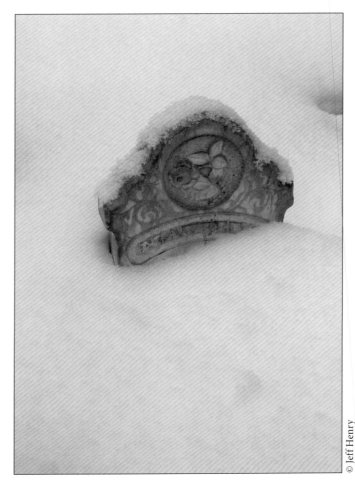

© Jeff Henry

Mattie Culver's gravestone at the mouth of Nez Percé Creek. In one of the saddest stories in Yellowstone's history Mattie succumbed to tuberculosis in March 1889 while winterkeeping with her husband Ellery. In addition to her widowed husband, Mattie also left behind her infant daughter Theda.

him, and afterward he yelled with fright whenever the novice orthopedics passed close by. A special effort to open park roads early, which was accomplished by hand-shoveling through deep drifts, finally allowed O'Connor to be evacuated to Mammoth a month or so after his injury. Special crampons, provincially known as "creepers," provide traction for winterkeepers walking on snow-covered roofs, and when they do occur, most falls land a winterkeeper in a deep cushion of snow under the eaves of a building. These factors together with skill and foresight probably account for winterkeeping's nearly injury-free track record.

Other tragedies have struck winterkeepers through the years, however. One of the saddest must have been the death of Mattie Culver, the wife of Ellery C. Culver, both of whom began the winter of 1888-1889 winterkeeping at the Firehole Hotel at the mouth of Nez

Percé Creek (the Firehole Hotel was the new name for the Marshall Hotel, where George and Sarah Marshall and their family had spent the winter of 1880-1881). Mattie died of tuberculosis on March 2, 1889, and in his isolation her husband had to place her body in two sawed off barrels to keep scavengers away until help arrived and a grave could be hacked out of the frozen ground. After Mattie's burial, Ellery had to finish out the winter in the Lower Geyser Basin while caring for the couple's infant daughter, Theda. Compounding the sadness of leaving the baby girl motherless was the fact that Mattie herself was only 30 years old, and she and Ellery were a month short of their third wedding anniversary. Mattie's gravestone can still be seen today, adjacent to the picnic area at the mouth of Nez Percé Creek.

Another sad story was the death of Christ Kassube, who died on December 2, 1902 while employed as a winterkeeper at Old Faithful. "Old Christ," as he was known, succumbed to some sort of intestinal ailment, and his case was sad because he was literally a very old man who apparently had reached the end of his string economically at the same time that he reached the end of his biological life. A series of communications from the soldiers stationed at Old Faithful and their superiors at park headquarters in Mammoth detailed the old man's decline. One of the first stated that *"The winter keeper stationed here in charge of the Hotel in need of medical attention Has been sick for ten days. We are doing all we can for him. We have no medicine."* Then later there was a communiqué that related *"I respectfully report the death of Old Christ. The winter keeper at the Hotel here....I can not say just what was the matter with him....He died of a stomach complaint....He sank rapidly the last three days. Could not speak the last two days And was unconscious all the last. Pvts. Hundly & Daugherty were sitting up with him when he died. I ask for instructions And what I shall do with the body."* Finally there was a transmission that said, *"I buried [sic] Christ the winter keeper here, as directed, Under a tree marked with a cross x About 100 yds southwest of Old Faithfull [sic] Tent. The body lies on the same side of tree as cross....We made a most thorough search [of the dead man's possessions] But failed to find any papers of any description Or any valuables [sic] Except $4.15 Which I will send in."* So poor Old Christ died in the snowy wilderness at Old Faithful, in the company of two army privates who were probably strangers to him, and apparently with only $4.15 to his name.

Tragedy struck Old Faithful winterkeepers again on April 11, 1927. On that date the Old Faithful Inn winterkeeper, whose name was Bauer, found some green plants growing in a thermal runoff channel. Understandably hungry for a new addition to the menu after a long winter, Mr. Bauer picked some of the plants and showed them to a park ranger naturalist named Charles Phillips, who was also living that winter at Old Faithful. Ranger Phillips identified the plants as a species of edible camas, and he and Mr. and Mrs. Bauer shared the greens with dinner at the winterkeeper house behind the Inn. A few hours after dinner, however, the Bauers were taken debilitatingly ill, to the point where they were down and absolutely out for a period of nearly 24 hours. By the next evening the couple were sufficiently recovered to go and check on their neighbor, but they found Ranger Phillips dead on the floor of his quarters. The plant the ranger had mistakenly identified as camas was actually the violently poisonous water hemlock. Significantly, the deadly plant still grows in great profusion along Myriad Creek, the geothermal stream behind Old Faithful Inn that runs right by the Old Faithful Inn winterkeeper house, which is the same house that was occupied by Mr. and Mrs. Bauer in 1927.

An anecdote that illuminates a brighter side of winterkeeping comes to us from Fern Barnard, who was the wife of the winterkeeper at the Old Faithful Inn during the late 1920s and early 1930s, or right after the Bauers had occupied that post. Mrs. Barnard wrote a wonderful little snippet about an idyllic winter afternoon and evening at Old Faithful in the December 1932 issue of *Yellowstone Nature Notes*, which itself was a wonderful internal publication of Yellowstone National Park in the first half of the 20th century. Fern spent the afternoon in question in the greenhouse that used to be located in the Myriad Group, behind the lower store and the lower gas station at Old Faithful. For many years a greenhouse (probably two different greenhouses, one succeeding the other) was maintained there to produce vegetables for the Old Faithful Inn dining room in summer, and was also used by the local winterkeepers for the same purpose in winter. Heated and irrigated with geothermal water, the greenhouse was able to grow produce all through the frigid months of winter.

By way of introduction, Fern related that "Three years of winter life [at Old Faithful] have been mine," and she added that her time as a winterkeeper's wife had been "Three years of delightful life, approaching earthly perfection." She wrote how she liked to snowshoe trails in the Old Faithful area, "where I find glory in the true sense," and went on to add more details about the natural environment, where the depth of the snow could be "twenty to sixty, seventy or more

National Park Service

Fern Barnard on her snowshoes with a ski pole she apparently used as a walking staff, outside the winterkeeper house behind the Old Faithful Inn. In some of Mrs. Barnard's writings, she expressed a preference for snowshoes over cross country skis. This photograph was taken in February 1931.

blast." On the way back to her house in the company of her dog she noticed a group of ten or more deer feeding on a green patch of geothermal ground surrounded by deep snow banks. The dog passed the small herd of deer "without a bark," and they also saw an old bull elk browsing a pine tree and a flock of geese flying overhead. Most dramatically, though, Fern could see telltale puffs of steam rising above the East Wing of the Old Faithful Inn, which told her that Old Faithful Geyser was in preplay and about to erupt. Writing in the present tense, Fern recorded what she did next: *"I hurriedly place my vegetables and flowers in our cottage, and as fast as my snowshoes can carry me, I hasten around the corner of the building [the East Wing of the Inn]. All is calm and the quietness of the evening permeates my very being. There arises Old Faithful, in all her winter glory, to meet the blue evening heavens. I feel humble and insignificant in its presence. I think of the thousands who, too, would thrill at this spectacle. Yet I seem to see through the mist and spring, the words 'For thine eyes alone.'"* Anyone who has ever been blessed with a similar opportunity to watch an eruption of Old Faithful when no one else is present can appreciate the feeling behind Fern's words.

A more lengthy and therefore more informative account of winterkeeping life at Old Faithful in the early 20th Century is found in a rare but marvelous little book titled "My Winter in Geyserland." The book was written by a remarkable woman named Beulah Brown, who in the course of her long life not only worked for many years in Yellowstone, but also taught school at several different locations around the United States, went to Europe in 1918 to entertain soldiers wounded in the Great War, was an important figure in the Girl Scouts, managed a hotel in Death Valley, and took a solo trip on a ship around the world in 1924 and 1925. Beulah had already worked in Yellowstone for seven summers, mostly as a guide for one of the park's camping companies, when she was approached in the summer or autumn of 1922 by a Mr. and Mrs. Musser, who were the winterkeepers at Old Faithful Inn. The Mussers had three sons and they proposed to Beulah that she serve as their tutor during the upcoming winter. As Beulah herself wrote, "I jumped at the chance."

inches, with the thermometer dropping from zero to forty or fifty below." These elements she contrasted with the greenhouse, where "inside I find a whole new world," a world where her fingers could "play in the fertile soil." Fern went on to list the produce she was tending in the greenhouse, a list which included lettuce, radishes, carrots, beets, potatoes, celery, mint, parsley, and even fresh flowers to bring some festive color to the inside of the winterkeeper cottage, which itself was heated with hot geothermal water.

Finishing her work inside the greenhouse, Fern hustled back to her living quarters, "hugging closely my covered flowers to save them from the wintry

Beulah began her book by describing the transition of the park from autumn to winter, which of course she did through the eyes of someone seeing the transition for the first time. She noted that the last workers, other than winterkeepers and rangers, pulled out in November, when they could still travel out of the interior of the park. Other observations included how train service to West Yellowstone ceased, and how Mr. Musser evacuated the family car from Old Faithful to West Entrance. Looking ahead, and apparently relating information given to her by others who had experienced winter before, Beulah noted how the winter temperature could be expected to drop to 50 below zero; that rivers in that park do not freeze in spite of the arctic temperatures because of their geothermal inflow; and that the roads were soon to be restricted to travel by those who knew how to snowshoe or to cross country ski (by this time the contemporary meanings of these terms had come into use). She also remarked on the improbable contrast of bare geothermal ground existing in such close proximity to deep snow banks and how it was always possible to hike on bare ground in the geyser basins, even when the surrounding area was covered by several feet of snow.

Soon after Mr. Musser had stashed his car in West Yellowstone, the predicted heavy snows of November began. As Beulah put it, "Then came the snow that bound us. For ten days it fell and each day I realized more fully that I was in, to stay. To tell the truth it was a queer sensation; I hadn't the calm feelings of Mr. and Mrs. Musser. I felt some kind of thrill---but then, that was my main reason for remaining." Wondering how she might spend Christmas that year, and pondering her state of isolation, Beulah observed that she would have to get better on her skis if she wanted to have much mobility, what with the snow already four feet deep on the level.

Beulah was especially impressed by how cleverly Mr. Musser had utilized what she called "geyser water" for the benefit of himself and his family. First of all, water was piped into the walls of the house, where the flow could be regulated to keep the house comfortable according to changes in outside temperatures. Ms. Brown also mentioned how geothermal water was used to heat and to irrigate the greenhouse, the same greenhouse Fern Barnard would enjoy about a decade later. In the case of the Mussers, however, the winterkeeper also piped the warm water into a chicken coop, where the chickens produced two dozen eggs a day, and also into their root cellar, where it kept their food stocks from freezing. Most cleverly of all, perhaps, Mr. Musser had laid the pipes for the warm water under the sidewalks that led between the buildings, so Ms. Brown and the Musser family always had snow free avenues to walk on the rounds to collect their bounty.

For Beulah, the winterkeeper's greenhouse was "like a taste of California; the air was warm and moist, and flowers and vegetables grew luxuriantly. Mr. Musser was continually planting, as we ate, so the season never ended." Much like the Barnards would do a few years later, the Musser family and their tutor used the greenhouse to raise radishes, lettuce, onions, tomatoes and cucumbers. Some of the latter grew up to two feet long, all while fierce blizzards blew and temperatures plummeted just outside the thin panes of greenhouse glass. Beulah added the tidbit that the geyser water they used to irrigate their crops was so hot that it had to be cooled before it could be applied to the plants.

Wildlife was present around the Upper Geyser Basin, but it seems not to the extent that we have seen in more recent times. Beulah Brown's little book notes the presence of mule deer around the Old Faithful area. She described what she called a "tame herd" and a "wild herd" of deer, apparently to differentiate between a group of habituated animals and another group not so accustomed to people. Judging from old photos taken through the years, it appears there consistently were habituated mule deer that wintered in the Old Faithful area; there are many photos of Old Faithful winterkeepers in close proximity to deer in the vicinity of the Old Faithful Inn, even to the point of feeding the animals from their hands or even out of

OLD
FAITHFUL INN
IN WINTER

JUST TO SHOW
MY SNOWSHOES
AND SKIS

Teacher, Yellowstone guide, and world traveler, Beulah Brown (left) wrote of her adventures during the winter of 1922-1923 in "My Winter in Geyserland." Pictured here outside the winterkeeper's house behind the Old Faithful Inn, Beulah lived with Winterkeeper Musser and his family

A close look at the photo of the Inn (above) shows conically shaped piles of snow under the architectural valleys of the building. The snow piles are the result of Mr. Musser efforts to clear snow from the roof.

Courtesy of National Park Service Library

MR. MUSSER
IN THE GEYSER HEATED
GREEN HOUSE

THE THREE
MUSSER BOYS

Winterkeeper Mr. Musser strikes a proud pose inside Old Faithful's "geyser heated" greenhouse (above), which Beulah noted was "like a taste of California."

The three Musser boys (left), whom Beulah Brown was engaged to tutor, also enjoyed a natural education in Yellowstone. Beulah noted that the Musser boys had lived their entire lives in the park, and had learned to ski almost as soon as they learned to walk.

Old Faithful's thermally heated greenhouse, pictured in 1917, supplied fresh, nutritional produce for isolated winterkeepers and their families.

their own mouths. A small herd of mule deer, varying between half a dozen to perhaps as many as 20, continued to winter in the Upper Geyser Basin until the late 1990s, when they abruptly vanished. Presumably the geyser basins did not offer adequate winter habitat for the deer after the reintroduction of wolves to Yellowstone, which happened in 1995.

Ms. Brown added other tidbits about wildlife in the Old Faithful area, saying that elk were occasionally seen near the winterkeeper house, and always seen whenever she or the Mussers traveled to Biscuit Basin, a couple of miles down the Firehole River from Old Faithful. She noted the presence of smaller species, such as rabbits (almost certainly snowshoe hares), weasels, minks and otters, as well as several different species of birds. In common with many observers since her time, she was surprised to see summer birds in the wintry geyser basins, including robins as late as December 21 and as early as the nineteenth of March. The geothermal warmed and bare earth of the geyser basins offers survivable winter habitat for summer birds as well as larger mammals, and in our time as well as in Brown's the surprise sighting of species like blue herons, kingfishers and snipes in winter is not all that unusual. Interestingly, Beulah also recorded that Mr. Musser saw a moose on Fountain Flats during the course of the winter, which at that place and in that season would have amounted to an unusual sighting anytime in the park's history.

Beulah progressed rapidly in the art of cross country skiing, saying that in learning the use of her skis and poles it was most helpful for her to watch the three Musser boys. The boys were superb little skiers,

who "had always lived in the park, and knew how to ski almost as soon as they knew how to walk." Skis in Beulah's time were still made of wood, usually hickory or ash. They were six to eight feet long, which was considerably shorter than the skis used by Yellowstone first skiers some 50 years before, at which time they had been up to twice as long. Beulah also used two ski poles, again in contrast to earlier days when only one long pole was employed. Her first ski trip of any length was to Lone Star Geyser, as it still is for many employees and visitors in the Old Faithful area today. In yet another indication that Yellowstone's winters used to be snowier than they are today, Beulah noted that there were five feet of snow on the Lone Star trail in early December. By today's standards, that would be a lot of snow accumulation even for some time much later in the winter. Another dated detail from Beulah's trip was that she referred to the route to Lone Star as the saddle horse trail.

Beulah used her new skill to explore the greater Old Faithful area, and she delighted in her surroundings. Her book is filled with passages such as these:

"On a clear day from the top [of the Howard Eaton Trail near Old Faithful], I could see the white peaks of the northern border, and with that view just filling my soul, to have then the swift ride through the green and white — well, I was, indeed, unspeakably thrilled....

"As we skied down the road past the steaming geysers, the whole basin seemed like a fairy land, every twig on the trees was thickly coated with frost or frozen spray and the sun from a perfectly clear sky turned all into one vast sparkle....

"The [Old Faithful] Inn, which is beautiful in the summer, when covered with snow was much more so; its many angles and gables were decorated by an artist who used white luster and diamonds, and who changed his design at the will of the winds."

The enthralled tutor was also impressed by the work of clearing snow from roofs. "Mr. Musser's work as winter keeper, consisted mainly of shoveling snow, and I have learned that there is a great deal of work to that, as well as an art. [Yes, Beulah Brown is the source of that wonderful passage.] "The Inn roof has many valleys which catch a large amount of snow, and these have to shoveled after every big storm. The smaller buildings have to be shoveled to prevent their falling in." Whether Beulah ever participated in roof clearing work is not clear, but given the attitudes of the time toward gender limitations, it is most likely that unfortunately she did not.

Beulah also used her skis in early February to make a trip to the town of West Yellowstone, a distance of about 30 miles, which she did in the company of Mrs. Musser. Clear, sunny weather on the morning of their departure excited Beulah at first, but the twenty below zero temperature that accompanied the clear weather made it "too cold for the skis to slip." The women delayed their departure until ten in the morning, hoping things would warm up and improve the gliding properties of their skis. But at ten o'clock the temperature was still twelve below, and they made it only to Madison Junction on their first day. There they stayed in a cabin, probably one belonging to the National Park Service, which was dark and, when they arrived, "colder than the out-of-doors, which was probably twenty below." Because of deep, overhanging banks of snow, they were unable to reach water in the river, so they melted snow on the wood stove. This is yet another hint that there was a lot of snow in those days — Madison is one of the least snowy locations in the interior of Yellowstone, and it would be quite unusual for the snow to have that much depth in the Madison area nowadays. The snow water melted on the wood stove didn't taste right to Beulah, so she made it into coffee. Then she paid a price for that because the caffeine kept her awake for much of the night.

Next morning the women set out from Madison on the way toward West Yellowstone. Another detail illuminating their time was that there was no packed trail heading toward West, at least not for the first mile or so of the trip. They did see a herd of about 30 elk along the Madison River a short distance down from Madison Junction. A ranger whom they had contacted earlier by telephone skied in from West and met them on the road at about the four mile mark out of Madison, and in his company and in the ski trail he had broken they all carried on to town. Beulah was struck by the appearance of West Yellowstone, which was buried in snow so deep that "the inhabitants were compelled to ski or [to] walk on a narrow beaten trail whenever they moved about." She further wondered what would happen if two heavy-set people "happened to meet on one of those narrow gauge highways," and added that "Children and dogs seemed to be the only real signs

of life." Mail deliveries that came three times a week from the railroad ninety miles away in Monida, Montana seem to have been a social focal point for the winter residents of West Yellowstone.

Some rangers from Riverside Ranger Station preceded Beulah and Mrs. Musser on the day that the women set off from West Yellowstone on their way back to Old Faithful. The rangers not only broke trail on the West Entrance Road, they also started fires in the Madison Station and had dinner ready when the women arrived there. Beulah wrote that the rangers had postponed their scheduled patrol to help out, and that after serving dinner to the women the men left to return to their duty station at Riverside, which was located on the Madison River just a short distance inside the boundary of the park from the town of West Yellowstone. Those rangers probably welcomed the chance to see some fresh faces, especially two feminine ones, but in any event they put in a long day, skiing something on the order of 26 miles round-trip as well as building those warming fires and cooking dinner at Madison. Beulah also noted that it had begun to snow in earnest by the time the rangers set out on their return trip to Riverside.

The snowfall had progressed to a full on blizzard by the time Mrs. Musser and Ms. Brown left Madison the next morning, so they decided to travel only five and one half miles that day, a distance that would take them to the Fountain Ranger Station. Even that modest distance became a major challenge, however, as *"The trail was entirely obliterated, and the drifts of the narrow road sloped dangerously toward the river.*

This January 7, 1935 photo shows a row of tourist cabins at Old Faithful heavily laden with snow, illustrating the need for a winterkeeper to remove the great weight bearing down on the structures.

National Park Service

A young cow bison on the roof of the Yellowstone General Store at Canyon in March 2008. Why this two-year-old female was alone is a bit of a mystery, but probably had to do with wolves that were in the area at the time and who may have broken up a herd. The bison seemed to want company, and climbed on to the roof over the 14-foot deep pile of snow that had been shoveled off the building.

Sawing very deep and incredibly dense snow-pack (above) into manageable cubes during the record winter of 1996-1997. Photo taken in February of 1997 at Old Faithful.

Lake Hotel winterkeeper Dale Fowler (left) shoveling a high valley on the hotel. Dale has spent 24 winters as a caretaker at Lake, and so has become one of the longest tenured winterkeepers in the park's history.

We bowed our heads and plodded on, little dreaming, however, that we were in the worst storm of the season....It was most difficult to see the telephone poles which were our only guides. Indeed, often in an unusually fierce flurry we could not see each other, and simply had to stand, digging our ski poles into the snow in order to remain upright. Every few feet we had to stop to rest, as we encountered huge drifts each one seemingly worse than the last. As we approached the station, the wind seemed to increase in its fury and I was afraid we would not be able to see the station, and might go on by. At last it appeared dimly in the distance — a distance of perhaps thirty yards. But it seemed like thirty miles because it was a real fight to make it. We fairly fell off the nine-foot drift in front of the station, onto the porch, took off our skis and opened the door."

After more struggles to make the station habitable for the night, the two women had a supper of bacon, bacon grease and bread. They went to bed early, as there was only a sixteenth of a candle available for light, but "the most monstrous rat of history, noisily appeared, and made the night hideous by realities." The rat was undoubtedly a pack rat, or more properly a bushy tailed wood rat, a species notorious for invading human living spaces and wreaking havoc on human belongings. Describing the rat's effect, Beulah wrote, "Indeed, when that rat jumped off a table or chair, the room shook and I shook with it." Needless to say, the women did not enjoy much sleep that night.

Leaving the Fountain Station the next morning, Mrs. Musser and Ms. Brown made it all the way back to Old Faithful. They had a near misadventure on Goose Lake, where they discovered only after they were out on the frozen surface of the lake that there were thin spots in the ice, which they attributed to geothermal inflow. The blizzard they experienced the day before was still blowing, and Beulah recorded that rangers later told her and the Mussers that the blizzard had formed a snow bridge across a hot spring that the women had skied across but had not broken through. The rangers claimed they figured this out by following the women's tracks sometime later, but without any question this story was either an absurd fabrication or at least an absurd display of ineptitude in the art of sign reading on the part of the rangers; presumably the government men were trying to impress or to gain attention from a single female. More believably, Beulah noted that it had snowed a foot and a half since she and Mrs. Musser had left Old Faithful, and therefore the trail was hard to find in places. Not only hard to find, it was also energetically draining to break through the new snow with their heavy skis and their tired legs. The winterkeeper Mr. Musser skied out to meet the women, which he did somewhere near Midway Geyser Basin, and from that point everyone gained from the broken trail he had made on his way out.

Beulah wrapped up her account of the junket to West Yellowstone by writing that "As we approached Old Faithful Inn, I felt more like singing 'Home, Sweet Home' than I ever did before. And after I had had a geyser water bath and a meal embellished with a green salad, I was almost ready to forget the woes of my recent past." Apparently the trip to West was Beulah's one big outing for the winter, as from all indications she remained at Old Faithful until May of 1923, when the roads were opened and she made a trip to Livingston, Montana. In Livingston she spoke to a Ro-

Jerry and Thelma Bateson pose outside the winterkeeper house at Lake Hotel one Spring in the early 1960s. Jerry Bateson was a kind and gentle man who spent 25 winters at Lake Hotel; from 1950 through 1975. Judging from their countenances, it is easy to see that the quiet, isolated life agreed with Jerry and Thelma.

tary group about her experiences during her winter in geyserland. She also wrote at least two articles about her winter adventures in Yellowstone for a newspaper in Livingston.

Elsewhere in My Winter in Geyserland Beulah Brown summed up the attraction of winterkeeping life, an attraction undoubtedly curious to many, when she wrote: *"Aside from the unique experiences incident to spending the winter in geyserland, there were other advantages peculiar to any period of isolation which I appreciated namely, time to do things, knowing that I could plan definitely and not be interrupted. So I read, and I practiced on the piano, and I kept my dresser drawers in order, and I darned my stockings. It gave me a luxurious feeling to be able to do these things."*

That's exactly it — winterkeepers and their families were surrounded by the incomparable beauty and wonder of winter in Yellowstone, and moreover they were insulated by their isolation from unwanted societal demands. Using snowshoes and cross country skis to move around, engaging in the heavy exercise of clearing snow from park buildings, all independently done in a clean, cold environment — it must have been an invigorating life.

Another remarkable aspect of winterkeeping in Yellowstone was that the nature of the life persisted through many decades, so that in many fundamental ways life for a winterkeeper in the 1950s or even the early 1960s was quite similar to what the life would have been in the 1890s. Only a few, slowly progressing changes had occurred in those intervening years, things like somewhat improved telephone service, the advent of home radio, and the installation of small, localized power plants at the various locations around the park that electrified winterkeeper houses and replaced the need for flame-dependent light sources. Other changes, also slow-developing in nature, probably included an increasing frequency of mail delivery, and a growing presence of park service personnel. Earlier in the park service period, rangers only rarely stayed the winter at duty stations in the park. As time went it became more frequent for them to do so, especially on the west side of the park, and most especially at Old Faithful. But for the most part, until the mid to late 1960s winterkeepers remained free to live their lives of quiet isolation.

Probably the biggest change in winterkeeping life, and certainly the most portentous, was the advent of motorized oversnow travel. Snowplanes first appeared in Yellowstone in the 1940s, and apparently were pretty quickly adopted by the park's winterkeepers. Snowplanes were mostly homemade contraptions that looked much like Everglades airboats mounted on skis and featuring enclosed cockpits. That is, they had a truncated airplane fuselage that usually accommodated two people, with the passenger seated directly behind the driver, and an exposed airplane propeller mounted at the rear of the vehicle; of course, fashioning a snowplane also involved removing the wings from the airplane fuselage. Snowplanes were capable of great speeds, reputedly up to 140 miles per hour, and they seductively opened up a great deal of new mobility for Yellowstone's residents. Trouble was, snowplanes also allowed people on the outside of the park to access the interior, and that improved access spelled the beginning of the end of the historic isolation enjoyed by winterkeepers.

Snowplane access was soon followed by snowcoach traffic that began to bring regular tours into wintry Yellowstone. Even more ominously snowmobiles, known in the vernacular of park residents when they first appeared as the "little snow machines," began to appear in Yellowstone in the early to mid 1960s. These improvements in transportation technology spelled the doom of the old winterkeeping life, and the evolution of oversnow transportation is such an important part of Yellowstone's winter history that it deserves its own chapter.

© Jeff Henry

The basic tools of roof clearing, a broad-bladed shovel and an old-fashioned crosscut saw.

Winter Transportation in Yellowstone

"Oversnow use has already been introduced and today's thinking includes the encouragement of this type of use in preference to [the plowed] opening of the roads."

© Jeff Henry

A classic Bombardier snowcoach in a classic winter scene in Yellowstone, with the Madison River and Mount Haynes in the background.

This chapter's subtitle was taken from an internal National Park Service document that was part of the planning process for the Mission 66 program as it applied to Yellowstone National Park. The Mission 66 initiative originated in 1956 and was a move by the Park Service to bring park infrastructure and management up to date in time for the agency's 50th anniversary in 1966. Mission 66 came about in part as a response to the surge of visitation America's national parks experienced almost immediately after the end of World War II. Because of the Great Depression and World War II, visitation to parks had been suppressed for more than 15 years, and maintenance of park infrastructure had been neglected for at least that long. After the war factors that included a much higher level of economic prosperity, increased mobility in the way of improved automobiles and roads, and

a large measure of pent up demand combined to bring swelling numbers of visitors to parks that were ill-prepared to receive them.

The problem of overcrowding in national parks occurred mostly in the summer season. One of the responses on the part of the park service was to try to spread visitation into other seasons of the year. This was one factor behind the push to open a winter season in Yellowstone, and to feature motorized transportation as a primary component of the winter season. This was a movement that can trace its antecedents back to the early 1940s, but which really didn't gather much momentum until the 1950s.

A recap of oversnow transportation in Yellowstone can be briefly told. Indians, of course, used some form of snowshoes, as did Euro-American trappers. Gold prospectors, who probably used snowshoes early on, graduated to cross county skis. Skis continued to be the chosen means of oversnow travel in wintry Yellowstone, with some marginally successful experiments with horse-drawn sleighs and dogsleds thrown in on occasion, until the 1920s. In the 1920s motorized conveyances began to appear on the scene. The evolution of various forms of motorized equipment in response to the problem of moving across deep snow is certainly the most complex part of the story of winter transportation in Yellowstone.

It is a bit of a mystery why there is practically no archeological evidence of snowshoes from the Yel-

Winter use of Yellowstone has evolved so quickly that almost any photograph of a cultural scene becomes outdated in very short order. This is a photo taken in February 1997. Since that time the park's major concessionaire has changed, so that logos on snowcoaches and uniforms on drivers are different. There have been major changes in regulations regarding snowmobiles since that time as well, so a duplicate photo shot from the same vantage today would not have nearly as many snowmobiles in frame.

lowstone area. The ethnographic record of snowshoes in the area is nearly as barren as the archeological record, but common sense would indicate that the Indians who lived in this area must have developed and used some innovation that allowed them to walk on top of the snow. The snowshoe was the response to the problem of moving over deep snow that was used generally in North America (as opposed to the ski, which evolved in Europe), so it is reasonable to assume that the snowshoe was also the adaptation that was adopted locally here in the Yellowstone area.

Snowshoes are made of organic and biodegradable materials, usually wooden frames with rawhide lacings, so they are prone to decomposition and that characteristic helps explain their absence from the archeological record. But there have been many archeological discoveries in sheltered caves in the area, where objects that otherwise would have been biodegradable have been protected from the weather and therefore have been preserved. A principal discovery of this type was Mummy Cave, along the North Fork of the Shoshone River just east of the East Entrance to Yellowstone National Park. Mummy Cave contained a marvelous assemblage of artifacts, including bows and bow strings, cordage basketry, and other objects made of materials similar to materials commonly used to fashion snowshoes, so if remains of snowshoes had been present there it seems that they would have been preserved as well. Mummy Cave is a relatively low elevation site in a river valley, but it is very close to a great deal of high country where snow accumulates to great depths in the winter. It would seem that the occupants of the cave would have had the need for snowshoes at some point during their use of the site, which dates back at least 9,500 years. This would be especially true when you consider that during that long reach of time there have been climatic periods that were wetter and colder than the present. But for some reason, evidence of snowshoes was lacking at Mummy Cave.

As far as the lack of citation of snowshoes in the ethnographic record of the Yellowstone area, absence of mention does not equate to an absence of the accessories in reality. Snowshoes must have been essential in certain places and at certain times, and the reason they were not specifically alluded to in journals or in other records of early times might have to do with the fact that they were so commonplace that their presence and use were assumed to be common knowledge. It might be somewhat akin to a contemporary story of a group visiting a back country thermal area in Yellowstone during the winter. An account of the story from a participant would probably have more to do with the geothermal phenomenon witnessed, or of wildlife seen along the way, than it would have to say about the skis that were used by the members of the party who made the trip. It would be assumed that the person to whom the story was being told would know that the trip had been made on cross country skis, that a pair of ski poles was used by each skier, and so on.

Cross country skis made their appearance in the Yellowstone area at least as early as 1872. As related earlier in the pages of this book, skis probably were introduced to North America by Scandinavians who became involved in prospecting and mining in the American West. As a very good answer to the problem of getting around in deep snow, the idea of skiing spread quickly, and at least some of the earliest prospectors in the area must have been exposed to the idea of skiing before they came to Yellowstone. It is probable that some of the earliest prospectors in the area may have used webbed snowshoes during the winter, but most probably switched to cross country skis in pretty short order, after they witnessed how superior skis are to snowshoes for most tasks that involve traveling over deep snow. In most snow conditions, for example, cross country skis are especially advantageous over webbed snowshoes for long distance travel.

At various times horse drawn sleighs and dogsleds were tried in early day wintry Yellowstone. Horses and sleighs seemed to work fairly well when there was a sufficient volume of traffic to keep roads broken open and packed down, as during the time when large amounts of freight were hauled to Old Faithful for the construction of the Old Faithful Inn, and to Canyon a few years later for the construction of the third Canyon Hotel.

Why dogsleds never really caught on in Yellowstone is another mystery. The snow in this part of the world, at least in high elevation areas like Yellowstone, is perhaps too deep and too powdery for dogs and dogsled to work well. The anti-dog bias of the National Park Service is probably another reason, although there are early photographs of park service personnel with dog teams and sleds, including at least one of the park's chief ranger Sam Woodring shot at park headquarters at Mammoth Hot Springs in the 1920s. The photos would indicate that the park service at least investigated the feasibility of dogsleds for use in the park. Perhaps the primary reason why dogsleds never really caught on was that Yellowstone is isolated from regions with more developed traditions of dog sledding. The region around Yellowstone was primarily horse country, and that is the tradition that was and still is

Yellowstone Mushers

Gene Day

Helen Day with sled and huskies at Riverside Geyser.

In early March of 1961, sled dog enthusiast Gene Day and his wife Helen from Idaho Falls, Idaho drove their team of seven huskies from West Yellowstone to Old Faithful on a whirlwind one day tour. This photo was taken by Gene of his wife in front of Riverside Geyser on their way to Old Faithful. Judging by the angle of the light in Gene's photo, the couple must have made good time on their way in from West and arrived in the Upper Geyser Basin in late morning. Indeed, in a recent interview Gene said his huskies did have "tremendous energy," and that the couple had to stop only once on the round-trip for their dogs to take a short nap.

The series of photos Gene shot on his 1961 trip clearly show the tracks of Bombardier snowcoaches, both on the open roads between Old Faithful and West Yellowstone and within the Old Faithful area itself. In keeping with the time of year, Gene remembers bare spots where the road passed through thermal areas, and it is evident from his photos that the snow is mushy from the spring sun, as one might expect from a clear day in mid March. Gene remembers seeing "a few people but not many" when he and Helen were at Old Faithful, and he also recollects that those few people respected one another's space and "didn't talk much with each other." The couple saw "some but not a lot of wildlife" along the way, and have one snap of a big bull elk along the Firehole River among their photographs.

The most dramatic moment of Helen and Gene's outing occurred when they were nearing West Yellowstone on their return trip. Someone had told the couple that they might see grizzly bears, and that the most likely place for those animals was around the town of West itself. In those days a lot of bears ate a lot of garbage at the West Yellowstone dump, and apparently bears emerging from hibernation were in the habit of making a beeline for the dump to take advantage of the bonanza that had accumulated there through the winter. Dusk was coming on as Helen and Gene were approaching the West Entrance that evening, and in the dim light the couple were sure they saw a grizzly cross the road in front of their team. A few moments of high adrenaline ensued, but the anxiety passed until a closer look revealed that the "grizzly" was actually a cow elk.

Gene and Helen's photos and account of their trip offer a nostalgic glimpse into a time in Yellowstone's not so distant past when things were simpler and more relaxed. Dog sledding was declared illegal in Yellowstone in 1982.

reflected by animal use within the park, where dogs are severely frowned upon and horses and mules are primary features of park subculture.

It's hard to say when the first motorized oversnow vehicle appeared in Yellowstone. The very first such creations were probably homemade contraptions that likely were cobbled together either in the park or in one of the nearby communities. It seems especially likely that the first cobbled-together contraptions appeared in either West Yellowstone or Cooke City. Deep, fluffy snow is a primary feature in both those gateway communities and because of the presence of a railroad in West and the mining operations around Cooke, there were able mechanics on hand in both

places. Winters were long in both communities as well, so any Rube Goldberg around would have had lots of time to come up with his own singular response to the problem of moving over deep snow.

The first commercial oversnow vehicle to appear in Yellowstone appears to have been the Armstead Snow Motor. This vehicle was unique in that it was mounted on and propelled by two large drums that rested on the surface of the snow. The drums were ringed with spiraled flanges that bit into the snow and augured the vehicle forward or backward depending on which way the drums rotated. For the sake of stability, the two drums spiraled in opposite directions, and the overall design appears to have been developed by one Fred-

Known in Yellowstone as the Screw Drum or the Screw Tractor, this peculiar vehicle was properly called the Armstead Snow Motor. Pictured here in front of the Lamar Buffalo Ranch, the Screw Tractor was used only on Yellowstone's Northern Range and only for a short time in the 1920s.

erick R. Burch of Seattle, Washington, who applied for a patent on his invention on November 27, 1920, and who was granted the patent on October 10, 1922. Mr. Burch apparently made some sort of deal with Ford, for some of the resulting machines used Fordson tractors as power plants, which were mounted on top of the rotating, augured drums. Interestingly, other varieties of the snow motor vehicles were fitted to Chevrolet car chassis. The Snow Motor designs appear to have been marketed nationally by sometime in the mid 1920s.

By January of 1926, the model had been out long enough to be featured in *Time Magazine*. *Time* reported that it was a machine "which will negotiate the deepest snowdrifts at six to eight miles an hour.... The machine has already proved its usefulness in deep snow previously unnavigable. One such machine has done the work which formerly required three teams." The article went on to list the snowy places where the invention was already being used, a list that included Oregon, Canada, Norway, Sweden and Alaska, and it added that the Hudson and Dodge companies "...are mentioned especially as interested in practical possibilities along this line."

At least two marketing films promoting the Snow Motor from the mid 1920s can be found on today's Internet. One shows the vehicle performing in deep snow in Michigan, and is about 11 minutes long. In the film shot in Michigan the Snow Motor appears to be quite maneuverable, and is also shown to quickly outpace a man asserted to be walking fast across the snow. Close-ups of the vehicle's spirally flanged drums show good flotation on top of the snow, with the flanges penetrating sufficiently to give good trac-

tion without slippage. The vehicle appears to be quite stable as it moves forward, reverses, and describes a number of deft turns. It appears that the vehicle was able to execute tight turns by engaging one drum in forward gear while simultaneously engaging the other in reverse. In this regard it was somewhat similar to a modern bulldozer, which can turn tightly by simultaneously engaging its two tracks in opposite directions.

A second film, also available on the Internet, shows the Snow Motor hooked to a sled loaded with a purported 20 tons of logs, with the location possibly in Oregon. Again, the Snow Motor performs well in the film, seeming to have no trouble pulling the heavily laden sled over what appears to be a packed snow surface. Its speed appears to be about that of some men walking alongside the load.

In Yellowstone the Snow Motor was locally known as the "screw tractor," or as the "screw drum." At least one of the vehicles was used to haul mail and other supplies between the Gardiner/Mammoth area and Cooke City, although it appears that it did so for only a short time. Photographs of it in Yellowstone show a model with an enclosed cab, something that does not appear in other photos or films shot of the machine elsewhere during the same time period. Perhaps the enclosed cab was fabricated on a custom basis here in Yellowstone, or in Gardiner or Cooke City, for the comfort of the driver on that long haul between the North and the Northeast entrances of the park. Without the enclosed cab the haul would have been very cold as well as very long.

Probably the second motorized vehicle of any consequence to be employed for oversnow use in Yellowstone was the snowplane. Unlike the Armstead

Leslie Quinn Collection

A snowplane (left) pictured at Mammoth in the 1950s is possibly a machine belonging to Lake Hotel winterkeeper Jerry Bateson. The snowshoes strapped to the side of the snowplane were an indispensable backup in case of a mechanical breakdown.

Snowplane pioneer Walt Stuart of West Yellowstone photographed two snowplanes arriving at Old Faithful (below). The foreground shadows are the silhouette of the Old Faithful Inn.

Leslie Quinn Collection

stead Snow Motor, the snowplane was a homemade vehicle fashioned by local handymen around the Yellowstone area. Its basic design was simple but effective, and therefore was quite consistent among the various mechanics who built them. In short, the vehicle was a wingless airplane fuselage mounted on skis with an exposed airplane propeller on the back that blew the machine forward in the manner of a modern airboat in the Everglades. The exposed airplane propeller was a dangerous piece of business, and at least one old time winterkeeper in Yellowstone bore a nasty scar on his back from being hit by the propeller on his own snowplane. The same man almost lost a finger to the snowplane propeller in a separate accident. Depending on the power of the machine and most of all upon snow conditions, astonishing speeds of up to an estimated 140 miles per hour could be achieved with these locally fabricated snowplanes.

Snowplanes appear to have come on the scene in Yellowstone in the late 1930 to early 1940s. As a sidebar, it is worth mentioning that the Great Depression may be one reason why the Snow Motor did not catch on for widespread or long term use in Yellowstone. Perhaps local people couldn't afford the commercial option of the Snow Motor, and instead turned to the homegrown solution of the snowplane, but that is just a speculation. What is certain is that by the mid 1940s snowplanes were well established in Yellowstone among the people who had the need or the desire to travel around the park's snow covered expanses in winter. Those people, of course, included winterkeepers, park service employees, and residents

of the park's surrounding communities. In retrospect, snowplanes were on the scene in Yellowstone for only a relatively short time, only a little more than 20 years, but that was long enough for the machines to carve out a niche in local lore. In the memories of people still living are great snowplane stories, including tales of ill-timed mechanical breakdowns on the road that resulted in long treks through the dark of night to get back home, and of crossing the ice of Yellowstone Lake at screaming speeds and looking behind to see liquid water welling up into the ski tracks of their snowplanes. At least two Yellowstone old timers related that when they looked in the tracks behind their snowplanes and saw open water, they always figured there was another layer of ice under the water, but that they never stopped to find out. Instead, they just kept on planing at speeds that, truth be known, were probably fast enough that they could have skimmed across completely open water without foundering.

For many decades the best option for snow travel was the cross country ski; as these rangers were using on patrol, circa 1920s-1930s.

National Park Service

Chief Ranger Sam Woodring testing dog team at Mammoth, 1920s.

National Park Service

A vehicle described as a "motorized toboggan" at Mammoth, circa 1939.

National Park Service

Jeff Henry Collection

Lake Hotel winterkeeper Jerry Bateson with snowplane on the ice of Yellowstone Lake. Jerry spent winters at Lake Hotel from 1950 through 1975, and he frequently used his snowplane to ferry NPS rangers across Yellowstone Lake, where he dropped them off for ski patrols into the country south of the lake. This photo was taken along the east shore of the Southeast Arm of Yellowstone Lake in 1963. With the skis, poles and pack laid out on the ice and Jerry stepping back into his snowplane, it seems likely that the ranger about to embark on patrol snapped the picture.

Snowplane and people with habituated mule deer by winterkeeper house behind the Old Faithful Inn, 1950s.

Leslie Quinn Collection

Early-day snowmobiles parked by the original Old Faithful Snow Lodge, early 1970s.

Leslie Quinn Collection

Tucker Sno Cats were used in Yellowstone by the NPS as well as by the telephone and power companies.

Another oversnow vehicle that made its appearance in Yellowstone in the mid to late 1940s was the military's M29 Weasel. The Weasel was the first tracked vehicle put to oversnow use in the park; its entire bearing surface was the propelling track, with no skis or rotating drums incorporated into the design. The vehicle was developed early during World War, originally intended for use against the Nazis in Norway, where ironically it was never used. Instead, it ended up being deployed on snowy battlefields on continental Europe. An interesting aside is that the strategy behind the plan to use the Weasel in Norway, as originally conceived, was designed with the idea that a few well trained troops equipped with the vehicles could operate on ice and snow fields and make quick attacks on key Nazi strong points. The strategy held that a great many Nazi troops would be tied down to defend widely separated targets from just a few mobile commandos. The tie in with Yellowstone is that the strategy originally called for deploying Snow Tractors to execute the plan in Norway. When it was decided

that Snow Tractors were not suited to the task, the M29 Weasel was designed in its stead.

From one government agency to another, surplus Weasels wound up in the possession of the National Park Service in the post World War Two period. Rangers used them to greatly improve their winter mobility, covering the distance from, say, Mammoth to Lake in just half a day instead of the several days that it heretofore had taken to make the trip on skis. The Weasels were apparently equal to their Yellowstone tasks, for they remained on the park scene, albeit at diminishing levels of use, into the 1980s. Park service employees found the Weasels especially useful during the days of elk reduction, when they used the vehicles to haul the carcasses of animals shot in the backcountry to park roads, where they were subsequently loaded onto trucks for transport, usually to regional Indian reservations.

Yet another tracked vehicle that appeared in Yellowstone during the post World War Two period was the Tucker Sno Cat. It was originally developed by a man named Emmitt M. Tucker who grew up in a classic background of a large family in a log cabin in snow country at a place called Jump-Off Joe Creek near Grants Pass, Oregon. It seems that as a boy Mr. Tucker had to walk to school through deep snow, and because of the memory that effort required he was inspired to develop vehicles in his adult life that could travel over deep and soft snow. Mr. Tucker was also gifted with mechanical ability, and after several failed attempts to solve the problem of flotation versus traction on soft snow, he came up with the design for his Tucker Sno Cat. Operating on the premise that an oversnow vehicle could displace no more weight per square inch on the snow than a person on skis, a displacement weight he calculated to be about eight ounces per square inch, he came up with a design that placed four independent tracks on the snow. His design also articulated both front and rear axles independently, so that his vehicle was extremely maneuverable. The Sno Cat was and still is used for work on both the Arctic and the Antarctic.

In Yellowstone, the National Park Service acquired a Sno Cat and found that it performed better in soft snow conditions, as well as in steeper terrain, than did the military Weasels. Following the National Park Service example, it appears that the telephone company serving the park acquired another Tucker Sno Cat to service their lines. Another important park utility, the Montana Power Company, acquired yet another Sno Cat to answer to their needs for winter transportation in Yellowstone. A principal drawback of the Sno Cat was its lack of speed. The vehicle could muster only about 15 miles per hour, even on the open road.

As time went on, other oversnow vehicles from other manufacturers were brought to Yellowstone, including models made by Thiokol, Bombardier, John Deere and others. In recent times at least two different companies from Europe have furnished oversnow vehicles to the park. One of the more unusual vehicles to ever appear in the park was a tundra buggy from Canada which was tested for possible use in wintry Yellowstone in 1982. Tundra buggies are used in Canada to ferry tourists around snowy or icy landscapes, such as on glacier fields in the Canadian Rockies and along the frozen beaches of Hudson Bay on polar bear viewing excursions. The buggy that was brought to Yellowstone in 1982 made its appearance at Old Faithful in the early spring after the park had closed for its winter season but before spring plowing had been completed. The vehicle was huge. The tires were larger in diameter than the height of a tall man, with the structure of the passenger compartment looming above that. It was also ungainly and painfully slow, requiring an hour and three quarters to make the one way trip from Old Faithful to Kepler Cascades, a distance of no more than two miles even by the roundabout route necessitated by the Old Faithful area's convoluted road system. Several of the park employees who had gone along for the trial run got off the vehicle at Kepler Cascades and walked back to Old Faithful, so slow was the trip. Officials in charge of the concessionaire's transportation division opted not to invest in any tundra buggies for use in Yellowstone, either then or later.

By 1949 winter travel with snowplanes had reached a point where a West Yellowstone resident began to offer winter tours of the park to the public. That resident was Walt Stuart, a fine and friendly man who had the distinction of having been the first baby born in the town of West Yellowstone, an event that occurred

Bombardier snowcoaches parked between the Old Faithful Inn and Old Faithful Geyser, with the world famous geyser erupting in low afternoon light. This photograph probably dates to the 1960s.

on August 15, 1909. Among his other attributes, Walt was an excellent mechanic, and he built at least three snowplanes of his own during the 1940s and 1950s. Park records indicate that 19 snowplane excursions with a total of 35 people made the trip in from West Yellowstone between January and March of 1949, although it is not clear whether all those people rode in with Walt Stuart, or whether another operator or operators also contributed to the total.

Whoever was conducting the tours, this development in winter tourism was momentous. Once started, it seems there was no turning back for winter visitation. Because of the distances involved in traveling through Yellowstone, as well as the difficulties inherent with moving through deep snow in a cold environment, it was inevitable that most winter visitation would be motorized. This was true whether the motorization took the form of snowplanes, snowcoaches or snowmobiles in the park's snowy high country, or in the form of automobiles on the park's Northern Range. As far as oversnow vehicles, which in the early 1950s meant snowplanes, the total number of visitors transported into the park increased slowly but steadily until the winter of 1953-1954, when a total of 171 persons rode the planes into the park. Most of this traffic was from West Yellowstone to Old Faithful.

In 1952 two West Yellowstone entrepreneurs, Harold Young and Bill Nicholls, purchased snowcoaches from the Bombardier Company in Quebec, Canada. The men thought that winter trips into Yellowstone National Park would be a "good tourist gimmick." The Bombardier snowcoach was the creation of Joseph Armand Bombardier, a French-Canadian who was a mechanical genius from a young age. His snowcoaches were squat, rounded machines that were driven by caterpillar-like treads under the rear-mounted engine, and steered by skis on the front of the vehicle. They were designed to haul a maximum of twelve passengers, featured heated interiors, and were widely used in Canada by the time Young and Nicholls bought theirs for use in the park. The unusual vehicles were especially favored in Canada for their efficacy in transporting children to and from school. Even today many of Bombardier's distinctive vehicles can be seen in cold and snowy Canadian communities. Churchill, Manitoba on Hudson Bay is one such example.

A contemporary Bombadier snowcoach remains functionally the same as its predecessors.

Young and Nicholls petitioned the National Park Service for a permit to use their new vehicles right after their original purchase, but they were not able to win a favorable response from the agency until 1955. The park service had a high degree of ambivalence with regard to the development of winter visitation, and moreover was concerned about the safety of park visitors riding into the Yellowstone on snowcoaches, which after all were new to the Yellowstone scene. Part of the original permit agreement between the two West Yellowstone businessmen and the park service included a provision that a spare snowcoach would always be on standby in West Yellowstone to rescue the passengers from any coach that might break down in the park. In another indication of park service ambivalence toward developing winter use, Young and Nicholls were permitted to conduct their snowcoach tours, but they were not allowed to advertise the service.

As a result of the snowcoach option, the number of visitors into the park who came via oversnow vehicle mushroomed to 631 during the first winter Young and Nicholls were allowed to operate their business. Numbers of winter visitors continued to increase slowly but steadily from then until the winter of 1962-1963, when there occurred an even more momentous event in Yellowstone's winter history. The National Park Service first allowed what was then often called the little snow machine into Yellowstone in January of 1963. Today we call the little snow machine the snowmobile, and with the advent of the machine to Yellowstone came another surge in winter visitation. The first full winter of snowmobile access to Yellowstone, that of 1963-1964, saw a total of 1067 oversnow visitors. Just seven years later, in the winter of 1970-1971, 19,429 people came into the park over its snow packed roads.

The first snowmobiles to come into Yellowstone in the early to mid 1960s were primitive affairs. Stories from the first people to snowmobile into the park are similar to stories from old timers who tell their tales about trips on snowplanes. There was a strong element of independent adventure involved with such travel in those days, with snowmobilers having to carry their own fuel and other supplies, and having to implement any necessary mechanical repairs with their own tools and with their own ingenuity on the side of the road.

That meant in the snow, no matter how cold it was, no matter how dark it was, and no matter how hard the wind was blowing — it was all up to you because there probably was nobody coming to help.

At the same time snowmobiles were appearing on the scene in growing numbers, business was increasing for snowcoaches as well. Nicholls and Young sold their permit to the Yellowstone Park Company in 1966. Immediately after acquiring the permit, Y.P. Company began operating snowcoach excursions out of Mammoth. That same year the company also decided to keep its Mammoth Motor Inn, now known as the Mammoth Hot Springs Hotel, open year round to accommodate winter visitors. From a business standpoint, opening the hotel on a year round basis in the late 1960s was an idea before its time, and there was not enough business for Y.P. Company to turn a profit from its winter operation. After four years of continuous operation, the Mammoth Hotel closed at the end of the summer season in 1970, and did not re-open for the following winter. The hotel at Mammoth remained closed in the winter until 1982, and even nowadays it is open for winter and summer seasons only, rather than operating on a year round basis.

Even without hotel accommodations at Mammoth, winter visitation to Yellowstone continued to grow, with most visitors to the park's interior naturally focusing on the Old Faithful area. By the winter of 1970-1971 the level of visitation at Old Faithful was overwhelming the services available in the area. Actually, the only service available at Old Faithful was a heated bathroom, where many visitors ate their lunches because it was the only heated building in the village. Some visitors, wishing to stay overnight in the Old Faithful area (or perhaps marooned there by mechanical problems with their oversnow machines) spent the night in the bathroom, again because it was the only heated building available. This situation of rapidly increasing winter visitation combined with other factors to bring about the opening of the Old Faithful Snow Lodge for overnight accommodation and other services the following winter. The opening of that facility and other attendant services in the winter of 1971-1972 mark the beginning of what could be considered the modern era of Yellowstone's winter history.

© Jeff Henry

© Jeff Henry

Snowmobilers riding two-stroke-engine machines spewing clouds of blue smoke, backed up at the West Entrance to Yellowstone in January 1995.

Yellowstone's Winter into Contemporary Times

XIII

"It is, therefore, the policy of the National Park Service to encourage winter use programs. The objective will be the maximum benefits possible to the largest number of people."

© Jeff Henry

Bombardier snowcoaches belonging to Xanterra Parks and Resorts parked in front of the new Old Faithful Snow Lodge.

For most winter visitors to Yellowstone nowadays the most salient feature of the park is the snow packed nature of its roads. With the exception of the 56 mile stretch of highway across the park's Northern Range between the towns of Gardiner and Cooke City, Montana, and a 33 mile stretch of Highway 191 in the park's northwestern corner, all park roads are closed to wheeled vehicles, and instead are available for traverse by tracked oversnow conveyances from about the middle of December until sometime in early to mid March. How this situation came to be is an aspect of Yellowstone's history not widely understood — not even among those with long associations with the park.

In the beginning, and continuing for many decades after the park's establishment, the technology to clear the roads of snow simply didn't exist. By the same token, technological contrivances that required cleared roads to operate didn't exist either, so there was no need for plowed roads. Beyond that, there was little demand for access to Yellowstone in the winter. National transportation networks were not as developed as they are today, and both national and regional populations were much smaller than now. People found enough outside the realm of Yellowstone to occupy themselves, and the park was largely a forgotten backwater during the winter.

A forgotten backwater in winter perhaps, but Yellowstone maintained a high profile in summer. By 1940, annual visitation to the park had grown to well over a half million, and local business people began to consider how much more profit they could make if visitation could be extended through the other seasons of the year. In that year regional business interests approached a Wyoming senator about pressuring the National Park Service into plowing Yellowstone's roads during the winter. The director of the Park Service responded to the request thusly: "Severe cold, sudden storms and the rapid changes in temperature make the Park dangerous in winter; drifting snow would make the roads treacherous; and it would require excessive outlays for equipment and manpower to keep these roads safe for travel."

Park service reticence combined with the entry of the United States into World War II, and for a time the issue of winter plowing of Yellowstone's roads fell by the wayside. Even summer travel to the park declined to almost nothing by 1942, and remained at very low levels for the duration of the war. For the World War II years Yellowstone benefited from a state of benign neglect in a manner somewhat comparable to the way the American West and its inhabitants were left alone in the early 1860s when mainstream attention was diverted by the American Civil War. To carry that analogy further, Yellowstone and its unplowed roads were left alone during World War II the way Plains Indians were left alone to hunt their buffalo during the Civil War.

Like the buffalo and the Indians after the Civil War, great changes came quickly to Yellowstone in the wake of World War II. By 1948 visitation to the park had topped one million, twice that of the pre-war record set in 1940, and pressure resurfaced to plow the park's roads in winter. This time the pressure came from a consortium of recreational groups in Wyoming, and government response was similar to that of 1940: "The standards of many of the existing highways were rather low, and not well-suited to plowing; the buildings in the Park's interior were not winterized; and plowing would be too hazardous." Yellowstone officials went on to summarize that "the proposal to attempt winter snow removal on the Yellowstone Park Highway System...is economically unsound."

Further pressure on the Park Service came in the form of an offer by a Wyoming contractor to do the plowing for much less recompense than what the agency had estimated it would cost to do the work internally, but of course no winter plowing program came to be. As time went on Park Service personnel advanced other reasons against plowing proposals, pointing out that plow cuts through deep snow would not only drift full during windy weather but also would block the view of park visitors as they drove through the park. Both of these were, of course, valid points.

The first commercial snowplane trips into Yellowstone began in 1949, and with only a few minor and temporary downturns in the overall trend winter visitation grew from that year forward. There were some pockets of doubt in Park Service circles about the way winter development was proceeding in its early days. Some of these doubts were questions about the safety of such travel, as expressed in quotes such as this one: "under present conditions, i.e., extreme isolation of this section of the Park in winter, we do not feel that the type of use...is desirable." There were also questions of how oversnow travel would impact spring plowing, as indicated by the park's superintendent in 1948 when he wrote that "the passage of several snowmobiles [not snowmobiles as we know them, but rather what today we call snowplanes] over the roads would pack the snow so that later freezing would leave a very hard layer of ice which would seriously impede the progress of our plows when they open the road. This would add materially to the cost of our snow removal operations." But by and large Park Service officials agreed with the direction of winter development, or at least tacitly consented to the way things were going.

As winter visitation grew, the commercial and recreational interests grew more entrenched, too, and the clamor for a road plowing program subsided as the interested parties were able to profit from the winter program as it was. At least the interested parties thought there was potential for profit in the future if winter development continued in the same direction. In later times, especially by the 1990s and the early 2000s, snowmobiling and associated activities became very profitable, especially for the town of West Yellowstone. Snowmobiling reached the point where economically it was carrying the town in the winter, to an excessive point in the opinion of some. When snowmobiling was curtailed it became apparent that West Yellowstone probably had put too many of its economic eggs in one business basket.

A Yellowstone Park Company sign dating from the late 1960s.

Because of growing visitation the oversnow constituency was able to fend off another round of pressure to plow park roads in the mid 1960s. By that time, snowcoaches had been on the scene for about a decade and the little snow machine, or what today we call the snowmobile, was making its appearance as well. Snowmobile advocates were becoming a significant component of the oversnow constituency. Illustrative of developments at the time were programs offered by snowmobile manufacturers to provide rental businesses in West Yellowstone with low cost machines that could be rented at correspondingly low rates to the visiting public for use in Yellowstone National Park. These programs were designed, of course, to develop the snowmobile business in the Rocky Mountain region generally and in Yellowstone in particular.

Another benchmark development in the mid 1960s was a conscious decision on the part of Park Service that it was in the best interest of Yellowstone to open the park to mechanized oversnow travel, rather

© Jeff Henry

The old Old Faithful Snow Lodge, served winter visitors from 1971-1998.

than to plow the roads in response to those lobbying for that option. The bureau's thinking was that plowing roads and opening them to automobiles was expensive and dangerous, arguments that had been advanced before, and that the level of visitation would not justify the cost of the effort it would take to keep the roads open. The Park Service also thought that plowed roads would primarily benefit local communities, rather than the nation as a whole, and again the cost from that point of view would not be justified. As far as opening the park only to snowshoers and cross country skiers, it was reasoned that only a very small percentage of the population had a level of fitness adequate to travel via those modes over Yellowstone's large distances. All these factors combined to ensure that Yellowstone's winter development would continue along the lines it had been following since 1949. That is, it primarily would be in the form of mecha-

nized oversnow day trips into the park with overnight lodging, at least for the time being, in gateway communities outside the park (principally in West Yellowstone).

When Old Faithful Snow Lodge first opened for the winter season in December of 1971, it was intended to answer the needs of a level of winter visitation that had grown to a point where over 19,000 people visited the snowbound sections of the park the winter before. It accomplished that objective, of course, but not surprisingly its opening also acted as a spur for still more growth. Winter visitation to the park jumped over 30% the first winter Snow Lodge was open, as compared to the winter before.

Negotiations held between the National Park Service and the Yellowstone Park Company leading up to the opening of winter services at Old Faithful apparently involved some discussion of using the area's most famous building, the Old Faithful Inn, for the winter season. Whoever introduced that notion to the conversation must not have had a good grasp of winter conditions in Yellowstone, and also must have had a poor understanding of the impossible challenges involved with heating such a cavernous and uninsulated building in such a climate. The Inn, of course, was not opened at that time, and never has been at any other time during the winter.

The Old Faithful Snow Lodge was a cinder block and clapboard building belonging to the Yellowstone

A photo from the winter of 1997-1998, the last winter the old Old Faithful Snow Lodge was used, with construction of the new Old Faithful Snow Lodge already underway. The old Snow Lodge was demolished and hauled away in the spring of 1998, and the new Snow Lodge was completed and ready for business by December of that year.

Park Company and located about a quarter mile south of its namesake geyser. It was situated in line with and immediately northwest of the Upper Hamilton Store, which in turn had been known originally as the Basin Auto Camp Store, a name derived from the nearby Old Faithful Campground. Before that first winter of operation and the assignment of the seasonal name "Snow Lodge," the building had been referred to as "Campers Cabins." The building served in summer as a registration office for a number of cabins that were located to its rear. Presumably the name, which seems like something of a non sequitur, was intended to draw campers from the nearby campground who might have tired of tenting, as in times of inclement weather. When the building opened as the Snow Lodge on December 17, 1971 it featured 34 rooms open to the public, with bathrooms down the hall. Those rooms had theretofore served as employee dorm rooms when the building was open as the Campers Cabins during summers. During that first winter, and for a few more subsequent winters, the small company of winter employees lived downstairs

in a back hallway, behind the laundry room. In all the years that the Campers Cabin building was in existence no one ever described it as attractive, no matter what its name happened to be. The Snow Lodge was somewhat winterized, however, and was the only feasible choice for winter use at Old Faithful at the time.

In addition to lodging, in its first winter of service the Snow Lodge also offered a dining room, a bar, and a small gift shop. Other services available at the lodge included ski and snowshoe tours and lessons, as well as snowcoach tours of the park; those services are still offered at Old Faithful in the winter today. A Park Service visitor center was open in the area, too. The visitor center actually had opened the winter before the first Snow Lodge season. Whether gas and oil were available to snowmobilers in the Old Faithful area the first winter that Snow Lodge was open is a bit unclear. Up until that point, snowmobilers carried their own supplies when they ventured into the park, and the best available information seems to indicate that they continued to do so that winter of 1971-1972. The very next winter Yellowstone Park Service Stations, Yellowstone's concessionaire for petroleum, did start a winter operation at Old Faithful, but company records show an entry of "No sales, No expenses" for the first winter of Snow Lodge operation, so it seems safe to say that the petrol company had no presence there that first winter. A check of the Old Faithful ranger log for that winter indicates that the Yellowstone Park Company did operate gas pumps near the Snow Lodge, but whether the pumps were designated for use only for company vehicles, or whether they were also available to dispense fuel to the snowmobiling public is unclear.

Beginning with that first winter of operation and continuing for many years thereafter, employees chosen to work at the Old Faithful Snow Lodge were a select group, the best available from the thousands who worked in Yellowstone's hotels and lodges during the summer season. In the early days the employees were indeed a select group, numbering less than 20 in-

dividuals. The size of the lodge staff grew as the years went by and winter business increased, but even in the late 1970s there still were only about 40-45 "Snow Lodgers," as they came to call themselves. Most of the employees in those times were young, energetic and excited by their surroundings in Yellowstone. Now most of the Snow Lodgers from those early days are in their 60s, and most of them remember the winters they spent at Old Faithful as the times of their lives. When they reunite nowadays, they predictably lament the direction the park has gone since their day, and they especially lament the state of today's winter employees at the present day Snow Lodge.

Park service employees at Old Faithful that first winter included three law enforcement rangers, although one of those three left for a full month in mid season to attend a school program in western Montana. There also were a couple of ranger-naturalists who staffed the visitor center, and a couple of main-

© Jeff Henry

A skier, a Bombardier snowcoach, and long-time snowcoach dispatcher Steve Blakeley in front of the new Old Faithful Snow Lodge.

tenance men to look after physical plant. It is apparent from Park Service records that the rangers were still figuring out management of the winter season as they went along. When Snow Lodge first opened in December of 1971, for example, the trail from the Old Faithful village to Morning Glory Pool was open to snowcoaches and snowmobiles as well as to pedestrians. By New Year's it became apparent that allowing oversnow vehicles on that path wasn't such a good idea — the turnaround at Morning Glory was a bit tight, for one thing — and the local rangers decided to close it. Then they had to communicate the closure to Yellowstone Park Company snowcoach drivers, who not surprisingly were disappointed by the closure. The rangers were more or less constantly roping off or otherwise barricading and signing other side roads for closure, as they determined which avenues were best to keep open for funneling the ever increasing flow of oversnow traffic.

In a portent that hinted at the controversy that was to come in Yellowstone's winter management, concession snowcoach drivers complained to Park Service administration about the Morning Glory closure, and they also urged the tourists on their coaches to do the same. This in turn peeved the rangers who had initiated the closure, who, in their ranger station logbook, described the snowcoach drivers as "...loud mouthed and empty headed." But the Old Faithful area's lead ranger was quick to reopen the road to Morning Glory Pool for Park Service oversnow vehicles when a Hollywood celebrity came to visit Snow Lodge during the holiday season. The lead ranger lost no time in inviting famous actor Charlton Heston and his family to go on a private tour to Morning Glory, with the ranger himself serving as tour guide and driver in a tracked Park Service machine large enough to transport the whole group. Who would be allowed to do what and where, especially with regard to motorized oversnow vehicles, would be the crux of Yellowstone winter controversy in the years to come.

For the next 22 years after Snow Lodge opened winter traffic and visitation soared upward, with only temporary downturns that were usually attributable to international disruptions of petroleum supplies, or to national economic slowdowns. Even these temporary downturns were relatively minor dips on the graph, and as everyone with even a

One of Yellowstone earliest snowmobilers, during the early to mid-1960s.

Jack Richard Collection • Buffalo Bill Historical Center

minor interest in national parks knows, controversy about winter management of Yellowstone grew right along with the growth in winter visitation. The primary focus of contention was, of course, over whether snowmobiling should be allowed in the park and if so, how it should be managed.

Winter visitation to Yellowstone peaked in the mid 1990s, when over 140,000 people visited the park each winter. Of that total, some 85,000 were riding into the park on over 70,000 snowmobiles. On certain holidays, especially during the holiday week between Christmas and New Year's and again on Martin Luther King's birthday in January and most of all on President Day in February, over 2,000 snowmobiles per day were entering Yellowstone. There were excesses beyond just the excessive numbers of machines. In the early days of snowmobiling in the Yellowstone region, the machines had been touted as vehicles to freedom, and as a form of masculine expression. Analogies were even made between snowmobilers and cowboys. In Yellowstone, some of the cowboying had expressed itself with off road travel and intentional harassment of park wildlife. On some of the busier days, the sheer volume of traffic on park roads (snowcoaches as well as snowmobiles) formed a barrier to any wildlife that might have desired to cross from one side to the other. Beyond all this, controversy over snowmobiling in Yellowstone seems to have boiled down to four areas — air pollution, noise pollution, conflict with wildlife, and conflict with other winter visitors to the park.

Early snowmobiles were powered by two cycle engines, and virtually all snow machines continued with the two cycle design until the early 2000s. Two cycle engines are innately very loud — think of the deafening snarl of a chainsaw — and very polluting. The machines lubricate themselves with oil mixed into their fuel, and inefficiently pass a lot of that oil and fuel in a raw state out through their exhaust systems and onto the snow. Two cycle engines also blow a lot of smoke. The incompletely combusted mix of fuel and oil they belch with their exhaust contains a breathtaking array of noxious chemicals, many of them known carcinogens. When a number of two cycle snow machines congregate or pass by a given point during periods of calm winds, they leave behind a greasy blue haze that lingers for a surprising time. Various monitoring programs sponsored by the park found unacceptable levels of air pollution in the wake of Yellowstone snowmobile traffic at places like the West Entrance and parking lots in the Old Faithful area.

Other research projects sponsored by the Park Service tried to determine the effects of high levels of traffic on Yellowstone's wildlife. To grossly summarize, some of these projects reported deleterious effects of snowmobiling on park animals, while others found that impacts were negligible. Predictably, results of such projects were heavily influenced by the evaluators' underlying personal attitudes toward snowmobiling. Yellowstone's Superintendent Jack Anderson, for example, was in charge of Yellowstone when snowmobiling was first permitted in the park. Superintendent Anderson personally liked snowmobiling and rode the machines himself in the park as

The blue haze of air pollution emitted from two-cycle engines hangs over snowmobiles just inside Yellowstone's West Entrance in 1995.

often as possible. A park service biologist directed by Anderson to look into the effects of snowmobiling on park wildlife reported, "...my field observations suggested that the elk that used areas near roads became habituated to snowmobiles.... Displacements of these animals was mostly confined to the road plus surprisingly short distances." By way of contrast, a young and fit graduate student from Montana State University looked into the same question in the same area just a few years later, and he concluded that "...snowmobiles harassed wildlife, displaced them from areas near snowmobile trails, and inhibited their movement across trails."

The contrast between these two points of view speaks to the underlying nature of the conflict over motorized use of wildlands in America in general, and to snowmobiling in Yellowstone in particular. Perspective in the matter is derived from interwoven elements like a person's age, economic status, educational background, social position, level of physical fitness, and whether a given person has privileged access to the park through some other avenue, such as employment and in-park residency. These factors

are also elements of personal and group identity, of course, and so are viscerally felt and tenaciously held. Debate on the subject of snowmobiling in Yellowstone quickly degenerated into one of defensive posturing and emotional extremism on both sides. Point of view based on pre-existing bias was so strong that a given person could look at a group of elk and decide that yes, they were being significantly disturbed by oversnow traffic, while another person could look at the same scene and the same group of animals and assert that the traffic was having no impact whatsoever.

Contrast in conclusion based on underlying personal attitude extended across the board. People who liked snowmobiling claimed that moguls on park roads were caused by snowcoaches, while people who drove or rode in snowcoaches declared the opposite. Cross country skiers who sought solitude by skiing away from the road claimed that snowmobiles were so loud that their noise penetrated far into the backcountry. True enough, especially in the days of two stroke snowmobiles, but others retorted that some snowcoaches, which likely were the vehicles that brought the skiers into the park in the first place, were louder

© Jeff Henry

Bison use the Mammoth Hot Springs to Tower Junction road to migrate to lower elevations, including ranges outside the park in the state of Montana.

than snowmobiles and that their noise could be heard at a greater distance from the road than could that of snowmobiles. Again, there was some truth in the counter argument, especially now in the days when all snowmobiles in the park are the much quieter four stroke variety. Ironically, at Old Faithful today the loudest sounds, and the noise that extends the greatest distance away from the village, are the vent fans situated on the roof of the new Old Faithful Snow Lodge.

Claims that oversnow traffic disturbed wildlife contained some truth, too, but again there was another side of the coin. Park animals naturally travel packed road surfaces, where the going is much easier than it is in unpacked snow off the roadway, and while traveling the roads are often pushed along by oversnow traffic. This unquestionably amounts to an energy drain for the animals, but others assert that the animals pick up an energy savings by traveling the packed roads at times when traffic is absent, as it is at night, so that the overall energy equation probably balances out or may even come out in the animals' favor. Other claims were made that wildlife off the road but within sight or earshot of traffic suffered disturbance. But at least one research project that evaluated wildlife alarm levels by analyzing chemicals found in urine the study animals left in the snow determined that they were more likely to be bothered by cross country skiers than they were by snowmobiles.

Other arguments asserted that groomed and packed road surfaces allowed for easier long distance migrations for park wildlife, principally with regard to bison. This argument maintained that at first Yellowstone bison used their improved mobility to better access various winter ranges in the park, and that as a consequence their populations grew. With greater populations came greater survival pressures, the argument continues, so bison were forced to migrate even greater distances, which ultimately took them out of the park and into the state of Montana, where they were usually killed by intolerant livestock interests. Counter arguments to this assertion include the fact that bison were directly killed by management actions within the park until about the time that oversnow recreation in Yellowstone began to take hold in the late 1960s, so prior to that time population numbers were held in check and there wasn't as much of a need for the remaining animals to migrate. There is truth to that, as well as in the further counter argument that in almost all cases park roads follow natural travel corridors, mostly along river valleys, that offer feasible migration routes to buffalo even if adjacent roads aren't artificially groomed. The last point is further

augmented with information gleaned from interviews with old time park residents, who recall that wildlife used park roads as travel routes even in the days when the snow on roadways was only slightly compacted from very light levels of human use.

In Yellowstone the controversy and the rancor increased along with the increase in winter visitation, and the upshot was an ever intensifying blizzard of lawsuits, counter suits, lobbying and other political jockeying too complicated to recount. The outcome of all the political machinations, of course, was that snowmobiling in Yellowstone was restricted beginning with the winter of 2003-2004. Restrictions included a requirement for the best technology available in four stroke engines, a daily quota on the number of machines allowed into the park, a nighttime closure of park roads in winter, and most significantly of all, a ban on independent snowmobiling. From that winter forward, at least so far, snowmobiling in Yellowstone has been done within the framework of guided tours, with each tour limited to no more than 10 machines. So itemized are the regulations that even the spacing intervals between machines are prescribed when groups are underway on the road.

Since 2003-2004 snowmobiling restrictions have continued with basically the same prescriptions, although there has been some fluctuation in the daily quota allowed to enter the park. Park visitors who wish to see wintry Yellowstone on a snowmobile now have to foot the extra cost of a guide, and are bound to the timetable and itinerary of a canned tour. To say the least, this is inconvenient for many. A couple of bird watchers, for example, can't expect their guide and the other eight people on their tour to wait with them until a certain species of bird shows up. And another couple who like to cross country ski can't snowmobile to a trailhead and park their machines while they ski into the backcountry. The situation has left many people wondering why it is acceptable for a wolf watcher to drive his SUV to Lamar Valley on his own to look for wolves, while another person can't drive a snowmobile on his own to Hayden Valley to watch the sunset.

Snowmobile rental companies in gateway communities around the park are also compelled to have guides on their payrolls, and to have them on standby even during times of slow business. And business is very often slow, with a marked drop-off in visitation since the new restrictions were put in place. The loss of winter income has hit many communities very hard. This is especially true in the case of West Yellowstone, Montana. Many people involved in the

Bison being pushed down the road by both snowmobiles and snowcoaches, along the Firehole River just downstream from the mouth of Nez Percé Creek.

© Jeff Henry

snowmobile business are perplexed by the way things have gone. In the beginning, complaints about snowmobiles focused on noise, air pollution, off road travel in the park, and excessive numbers of machines.

Now, with four stroke machines, the issues of noise and air pollution have largely been answered. Off road travel, which has always been illegal in the park, is now virtually impossible in Yellowstone's powdery snow as four stroke machines have an inadequate power to weight ratio. Off-roading with a four stroke machine is almost certain to get a rider stuck, and once stuck the four stroke machines are so heavy that it is nearly impossible for a person acting alone to extricate one of them and get it back on the road. Finally, with daily caps on the number of snowmobiles allowed into the park the issue of overcrowding has been addressed as well. Many rental businesses feel they made a genuine and sincere effort to comply with the requirements for new snowmobile technology, and then were left holding the bag with a large investment in new four stroke machines that could not be rented frequently enough to pay for their outlay.

Within the park there are many who have gained a new appreciation for the fact that snowmobiles really can be useful machinery. It is one thing to idealize a non-motorized park, for example, but it is quite another to be an employee who has to travel from Old Faithful to Grant Village to read the meter on a propane tank, and to perform the task within the structure of modern day time frames. A similar statement could be made regarding a park employee's need to travel out of the park for groceries or other supplies. Proposals to organize communal transportation utilizing large oversnow vehicles capable of transporting a number of employees on the same trip have run up against the realization that it is very difficult to coordinate disparate schedules, especially when factoring in the long travel times engendered by slow moving tracked vehicles and Yellowstone's distances.

Of course, there are those who view the diminution of snowmobile numbers as all to the good, regardless of any downsides that may be involved. Many envision a winter operation where all visitors ride into Yellowstone on snowcoaches, and snowmobiles are entirely banned from the park. The increase in demand for snowcoaches has led to several new innovations in recent years, and generally snowcoaches have been getting larger in expectation that demand for that form of transportation will grow in the future. Expenses involved in traveling into the park on snowcoaches are considerable, and there are persistent complaints that

visiting Yellowstone in winter has been priced out of the range of most Americans.

Various proposals are presently being considered by the National Park Service for long term winter management. They include one that would phase out all snowmobile use in favor of snowcoaches; another that would restore some provision to allow for independent snowmobile travel; and still another proposal which would eliminate both snowmobiles and snowcoaches — a measure that would, of course, effectively end winter use of Yellowstone's interior. And that dredges up an idea from Yellowstone's past in that it would allow for plowing of some of the park's interior roads, mainly those on the west side of the park.

The most likely plowing scenario would open the road from West Yellowstone to Old Faithful, and possibly from Mammoth to Old Faithful as well. The plowed roads then would be open only to commercial wheeled vehicles — they would not be open for private cars. This development would perhaps solve some problems in winter management — it might be a little less expensive to ride a wheeled van from West Yellowstone to Old Faithful, for example. Of course, the measure would also create a suite of new problems. One of the biggest would be how to handle the interface where the wheeled vehicles meet oversnow vehicles. Presumably this would mean plowing a large parking lot at Old Faithful, where wheeled vehicles could maneuver and park. Another lot would have to be plowed in the Norris area, where wheeled vehicles could meet snowcoaches that would pick up visitors there for tours on the east side of the park. The wintry face of Yellowstone would look quite different in these scenarios. And of course a wild card here is the world's changing climate. If Yellowstone's climate becomes warmer and dryer, and there are indications that may be what is happening, then debate about how to manage winter transportation in the park may be rendered moot. Time will tell.

Bison captured and corralled when trying to migrate out of the park near Gardiner, Montana.

End of winter, 1922, a road crew clears a big drift at Golden Gate.

About the Author...

True to the diversity Yellowstone Country demands of its residents, author and photographer Jeff Henry has worked in Yellowstone National Park as a seasonal ranger, fire-fighter, fishing guide, wildlife researcher and winterkeeper while pursuing a career as a professional freelance photographer and writer.

Jeff's photographs of Yellowstone Park and the Greater Yellowstone area have graced the pages of national publications for over thirty years. Winter has long been Jeff's season of preference; a passion he publicized in two books, *The Yellowstone Winter Guide,* revised in 1998 and *Yellowstone Winterscapes,* released in 2000. In 2004, Jeff collaborated with Karen Wildung Reinhart in the publication of *Old Faithful Inn: Crown Jewel of National Park Lodges* to commemorate the centennial of the famous inn.

Jeff continues to maintain a personal relationship with Yellowstone snow as a winterkeeper. During the off-seasons, he lives and works at his home on the banks of the Yellowstone River with his daughter, Mariah.

— *Jerry Brekke*